CLERGY FAMILIES

CLERGY FAMILIES

Is Normal Life Possible?

PAUL A. MICKEY & GINNY W. ASHMORE

ZondervanPublishingHouse
Academic and Professional Books
Grand Rapids, Michigan

A Division of HarperCollins*Publishers*

Clergy Families: Is Normal Life Possible?
Copyright © 1991 by Paul A. Mickey and Ginny W. Ashmore

Requests for information should be addressed to:
Zondervan Publishing House
Academic and Professional Books
1415 Lake Drive S.E.
Grand Rapids, Michigan 49506

Library of Congress Cataloging-in-Publication Data

Mickey, Paul A., 1937-
Clergy families : Is normal life possible? / Paul A. Mickey
and
Ginny W. Ashmore.
p.   cm.
Includes bibliographical references.
ISBN 0-310-53561-1
1. Clergy–Family relationships. I. Ashmore, Ginny W.
II. Title.
BV4396.M53 1991
253'.2–dc20   91-14817
                                                          CIP

Edited by Robert D. Wood
Cover Designed by Terry Dugan

Printed in the United States of America

91 92 93 94 95 / CH / 10 9 8 7 6 5 4 3 2 1

Contents

154

Acknowledgments

We wish to thank those in the various denominations who assisted us in the sample, selection, and distribution of the survey materials. Our gratitude is extended to the hundreds of pastors of local churches who took time to complete the questionnaire and to talk with us about their ministry and their families.

We are indebted to our colleagues at Duke University with whom we have discussed the research design, the findings, and their implications. We are especially grateful to attorneys John Boley and Thomas Robinson, who gave up their law practice to pursue ministry and who helped formulate the concepts and wording of chapter five.

The J. M. Ormond Center for Research and Development at Duke University has supported the project through both funding and time so that we might pursue our interests to this stage of publication.

To Michael Smith and Stanley Gundrey of Zondervan Publishing House we express our thanks for recognizing, in the embryonic stages of the project, its promise for ministering to ministers and the church.

Finally, to our families who have surrendered their claims to our time and energy in order to make possible a project that is both complicated and time consuming we say, "Thank you."

Paul A. Mickey
Ginny W. Ashmore

7

Foreword

Through most of the twentieth century the clergy family has resisted many of the social, marital, and sexual pendulum swings of family instability in the larger culture. The pastor's family was expected to be an example of Christian grace and togetherness, a witness to society of what a family ought to be. Protestant clergy were expected to maintain monogamous, lifelong marriage commitments. Clergy family members were seen to embody and practice the virtues of the Christian faith as taught by their denomination. Today, however, families in general—including clergy families—are threatened by a rising divorce rate, a declining birthrate, and a growing proportion of wives and mothers employed outside the home. The minister and family are caught between what an American Christian was expected to be in the late nineteenth century and the sometimes grim familial and economic realities that encompass most marriages in the late twentieth century.

Since the 1960s, the clergy family has come under increasing pressure from forces operative in the larger society. Changes that have occurred in today's parsonage, manse, or rectory families are obvious even to the casual observer. Far fewer such families consist of the minister husband, the homemaker wife, and the statistical 2.3 pleasant children. Most pastors' spouses are employed—and at times at a better income than that provided by the congregation. A growing number of ministers are single women. During the past two decades we have witnessed the emergence of the clergy couple where both husband and wife are ordained, usually with each pastoring a different congregation.

In the 1960s, divorce among ministers was not acceptable. As recently as 1980 divorce virtually assured that the pastor involved would leave the ministry or at least cease to continue as a pastor. This was true in virtually all denominations and is still the case in some today. The divorce rate continues to increase among Protestant clergy, but is now generally accepted in mainline denominations as a sad but not spiritually disqualifying experience for a minister. The acceptance of divorce among the clergy is illustrated by the fact that since 1980 the United Methodist Church has elected several divorced clergy to the office of bishop.

These gradual and often-cited changes may appear insignificant for society at large. Pressures on marriage and family rising from emergence of the dual-career marriage, marriages in which the partners share the same profession, the second career, and the nearly universal use of day-care services for preschool child care for working parents are obvious realities. But even more pronounced and traumatic is their impact on the minister and the minister's family as well as in the thoughts and actions of local church lay leadership (deacons, vestry, session, pastor-parishioner relations committees, pulpit committees, and governing boards) who understand that part of their Christian vocation is to provide loving and authentic supervision and care for the pastor and the pastor's marriage and family. The clergy family has indeed crossed a threshold of new and highly conflicted expectations. The task of living as a clergy family and being involved with and employed as pastor of a congregation is immensely complicated.

Other examples could be cited to indicate that the clergy family is in a period of radical transition, a transition as profound as the introduction of married clergy by the Protestant Reformers in the sixteenth century. The sheer complexity is further strained by the increasing level of frustration and conflict over the "proper" lifestyle, behavior, and attitudes espoused by clergy as a model Christian family in a highly visible church leadership role. Traditional roles seem no longer to apply. Confusion and frustration among clergy, their spouses, and the lay members abound.

To examine the clergy family in contemporary Protestant churches, the J. M. Ormond Center of Duke University Divinity School conducted a nationwide study of pastors of local churches in eleven Protestant denominations. The purpose was to consider how the role of pastor affects the family, how the spouse affects his/her partner's ministry, and how being in the ministry influences the clergy family.

The material in this book is based in part on that survey. The denominations represented a wide range of churches and included American Baptist Churches in the U.S.A., the Assemblies of God, The Christian Church (Disciples of Christ), Church of God (Anderson, Indiana), Church of the Nazarene, The Episcopal Church, Evangelical Lutheran Church in America, The Presbyterian Church in America, Presbyterian Church U.S.A., United Church of Christ, and The United Methodist Church. Questionnaires were mailed to 1,446 ministers. Responses were received from 52.6 percent of them. Respondents were asked to give their names and phone numbers if they were willing to be interviewed by phone. Approximately half did so, making it possible to conduct follow-up interviews with some. The material in this book represents the thinking of today's pastors about the joys and satisfactions as well as the problems and frustrations that the ministry causes for their families.

Paul A. Mickey and Ginny W. Ashmore bring two somewhat different but complementary perspectives to their analysis. Dr. Mickey is a United Methodist with long experience as a pastor, pastoral counselor, and seminary professor. Mrs. Ashmore is a Presbyterian and a pastor's wife who brings the viewpoint of the present younger generation of church leaders.

The authors set the clergy family in a historical perspective, showing how the present state of affairs developed and has been influenced by events in the recent and more distant past, how the individual's theological call to ministry is related to the clergy family, and the sources of tensions and of satisfactions for the clergy family. The authors make extensive use of metaphors throughout the book to present their findings and to assist the reader more easily to understand the material. Although the analysis that Professor Mickey and Mrs. Ashmore present is based on an extensive survey, their manner of presenting their findings makes for lively reading.

This book will help pastors and their spouses understand and cope with issues affecting the Christian church and its ministry. These materials will be of great value to lay officials and members of local congregations who share with the pastor the responsibility for the ministry of their church. Finally, denominational officials will find these data helpful as they work with both pastors individually and with the congregations that constitute the body of Christ.

Data gathered in the survey confirm what is generally assumed. Great changes are occurring in clergy families of the Protestant churches across America. What happens in those families profoundly affects the way ministers perform their task. Only by clearly understanding these changes can appropriate action be taken. This book makes a significant contribution to that understanding.

Robert L. Wilson, Director
J. M. Ormond Center
The Divinity School
Duke University

1

Snapshots of the Clergy Family

In this chapter, we will sketch a historical glimpse or take a snapshot of clergy families throughout the history of the church. This approach allows us to view the many features of the clergy family that various people presume to be essential, while later periods may judge earlier aspects as old-fashioned or out-of-date, or even in need of recovery. Through these brief historical narratives, we can begin to understand both where we have come from and where some of our contemporaries think we might, or should, be going.

We begin with the Roman Catholic priesthood that held to vows of celibacy. In Protestant circles of the sixteenth to eighteenth centuries, marriage was seen as a theological statement in opposition to the false Roman view of celibacy, not merely as a matrimonial arrangement. A second era emerges by the nineteenth to mid-twentieth century among clergy families. They emphasized ways ministers' wives conducted themselves in the home, church, and public. The third distinct period is seen from the 1950s on and reveals the stress and confusion seen frequently among more recent clergy marriages that expand to include women ministers, dual career couples, and divorced clergy.

From Biblical Times to the Reformation

The history of clergy marriage is long and diverse. Many leaders in both Old and New Testaments were married. In the

Old Testament were Adam and Eve, Abraham and Sarah, and King David and King Solomon who also had concubines. Jeremiah (Jer. 16:1-4) apparently chose, as a sign of his prophetic ministry, not to marry and procreate. In the New Testament, especially for Jesus and St. Paul, the question of marriage is much more complex. Popular and traditional beliefs maintain that neither Jesus nor the apostles were married. St. Paul's advocacy of celibacy and refraining from marriage are seen theologically; that is, with the anticipated imminent return of Christ, he believed it best not to marry. However, as a Pharisee, we may assume that Paul had fulfilled his "religious obligation for a pious Jew,"[1] a belief apparently shared by Clement of Alexandria, Origen, Eusebius, and even Ignatius.[2] Perhaps St. Paul was widowed or divorced.[3]

The reader will need to choose between a popular cultural notion and a technical biblical and historical exegesis of the basis for biblical perspectives on marriage. One may choose to hold a position advocated by St. Paul or one may be concerned about the end times and choose celibacy because of the practical sexual value of not being open at all, for theological reasons, to sexual activity. Both the eschatological (the kingdom is coming) and the sexual-control positions reject the procreational expectations embedded in the early Judeo-Christian traditions. While no substantial biblical or non-canonical evidence can be convincingly marshaled to support a belief that Jesus ever married, as with St. Paul it would have been expected.[4] However, Jesus' teachings about sexuality and marriage (Matt. 5:27–28; 19:4–6) and divorce (Matt. 19:9; Mark 10:11–12, Luke 16:18), coupled with references to women disciples (Matt. 27:55; Mark 15:40; Luke 8:1–2), suggest that Jesus held radical views toward sex, marriage, women, and divorce. Women were welcomed into the kingdom as disciples, followers, and spiritual equals. Further, Jesus' teachings on marriage and divorce make the point that in the kingdom of God men may no longer act capriciously toward women by simply issuing certificates of divorce; rather, men as well as women are held to the same obligation under Jewish law to honor the marriage relation.[5] In the cumulative wisdom of the New Testament as developed in Roman Catholic tradition, the ideal and preferred status for clergy of the church is the single, celibate life.

The early theological rationale about the clergy and marriage and sex suggests that Christian marriage is comparable to the mystery of Christ's presence in the church and in the lives of believers. Martellet writes, "The identity of the church does not depend just on the power of men, but on the love of Christ that apostolic preaching never ceases to proclaim and to which we adhere through the outpouring of the Spirit."[6] The church becomes a sacrament and the source of the sacramental nature of marriage because the church is seen as the spouse of Christ. The "marital unity" of Jesus and the church is often explicit in Pauline writings (especially Eph. 5; 2 Cor. 11:2). Jesus becomes "the perfect bridegroom" (Col. 1:18; 1 Cor. 15:14; Matt. 22:1–10; 25:1–12). A husband and wife in the Roman Catholic tradition play out the sacramental nature of their marriage through the union they seek in the marriage ceremony. The invisible mystical union becomes visible in the physical union. The church teaches that "the mystery proper to Christ as the bridegroom of the church shines forth and can shed light upon the couples that are consecrated to him. . . . Their conjugal love . . . refers back to the love of Christ who supports and sustains them . . . [and] makes it possible for the love of the couple to become the image of the love of Christ for the church."[7]

The Roman Catholic Church came to see herself to be the spouse of Christ, and that relationship is sanctified as Christ's love is perfected within and made visible by marriage. When Protestant groups decided to permit clergy marriage, a similar theological conclusion became evident: if Christ is the perfect bridegroom, the clergyman must also be the perfect bridegroom for his wife as well as for the church. Thus the church as local congregation becomes his spouse through ecclesial means. The Roman Catholic Church dealt with this theological problem of "triangulation"[8] in its demand that clergy must live celibately, being married to only one: the church that is the visible presence of Christ. And only the church can bless the marriage union.

One theme that Roman Catholicism contributes to the theological development of clergy families is opposition to birth control and abortion based upon the biblical axiom to "be fruitful and multiply." This teaching is to be lived out through procreation by the laity, but the clergy are restricted to spiritual fruitfulness. Not only did Martin Luther marry, but in his effort to live out the priesthood of all believers, he influenced

Protestant clergy to abandon or overthrow the Roman Catholic notion that the spiritually perfect priest is married to the church rather than to a human being. The Protestant transition toward a married clergy was not simple or easy. Preindustrial agrarian society had been a natural support for the Roman Catholic theology of the extended family. The Anglican, Reformed, and Wesleyan movements began to challenge conventional Roman Catholic views of marriage and family from a sociological as well as theological perspective.[9]

In Martin Luther's protest against Roman Catholicism, he declared that marriage for the clergy and true believers was not a means of grace but a way of life. Sacramental intimacy with Christ is not through marriage but by faith. A celibate priesthood was theologically out of order for the Reformers. Luther advocated the marriage of clergy as a proper biological one. Margaret H. Watt cites Luther's observations that "the principle of marriage runs through all creation, and flowers as well as animals are male and female."[10] Luther was also eager to advance a theological claim by advocating marriage among clergy: "[The doctrine of celibacy] is an invention of Satan. Before I took my wife I had made up my mind that I must marry someone and had I been overtaken by illness, I should have betrothed myself to some pious maiden."[11] But the Roman Catholic notion of the clergy being unencumbered by worldly cares, particularly those of family, persisted. During the English Reformation of the sixteenth century, "imprisonment, loss of property, or hanging were provided for those who dared break the vows of celibacy to take a wife."[12]

During the ecclesial upheavals of the mid-sixteenth century, Archbishop Thomas Cranmer was burned at the stake (1556) by Queen Mary. He, like Luther, had married in Germany in 1533, six years before the Act of Six Articles, which was designed to enforce celibacy and thwart clergy marriage. If Cranmer's wife were to accompany him on his duties as archbishop, she had to be transported from one place to another in a "traveling box, replete with ventilating holes."[13] Cranmer's wife cramped up in a "coffin with breathing holes" in order not to be seen in public while accompanying her husband on his clerical travels is a powerful image. It casts a long shadow. For some today, however, the emotional trauma of being a clergy spouse is similar to that of Mrs. Cranmer.

As Protestantism spread to the American colonies and later throughout the United States, significant changes occurred in the role and public perception of the minister's wife. Whereas in the Roman Catholic tradition, the Virgin Mary was an object of veneration and esteem for her "Vessel-of-Honor" role in giving birth to the Son of God, we know little about Mary as an individual, a mother, or a wife. Therefore, the female role models within Roman Catholicism clustered around the virgin vessel typology (somehow inspiring, for example, the great cathedrals) or around the martyr typology, such as Jeanne d'Arc, the soldier; or Teresa of Avila, the mystic. These women provided no guidance for the routine tasks of the pastor's wife in the rectory, parsonage, or manse because neither was married to a pastor.

In Protestantism the theological role of the minister shifted away from the more spiritual beatific one associated with female saints in the Roman Catholic Church. Several distinct features were retained in the typical portrait of clergy families of the nineteenth and twentieth centuries. These themes suggest that the woman is to live a pure virginesque social and sexual life, that she is to expect a life of martyrdom—not to the enemies of the church but to her husband's career as she gives total support to his ecclesial adventures. And, finally, she is to be diligent in season and out of season. She is to work somewhat like the women mystics who regarded the quietness of meditation, solitude, and hard physical labor as a means by which purgation is achieved and unity with the will of God realized.

Manuals for rectors' or pastors' wives appeared by the early nineteenth century. The following admonitions are typical: "Beyond all doubt, the keystone in the fabric of the rectory system is marriage, a happy and harmonious marriage. . . . Edward Stanley's marriage to Catherine Leychester in 1810 made possible all his long years of exemplary domestic life and ministry."[14] By the end of the eighteenth century and in the early nineteenth, the elevated role of the clergyman as a person of commerce, industry, jurisprudence, and civil authority in American society had shifted to more purely religious and liturgical functions. The beginning stages of pastoral care linked up with the social reform movement of the late eighteenth century, whose key figures were women. Ann Douglas, in her classic work *The Femininization of American Culture*, details the alliance of the clergy with women reformers. In her chapter "Ministers and Mothers: Changing and Exchanging Roles," she claims that both groups sentimentalized life: "As the century wore on, [the clergy] were described more and more frequently by themselves and by contemporaries in terms that stressed their softer susceptibilities."[15]

The typical clergy family takes on a character of dramatically different hues and tones by mid-twentieth century. Many books were published as helpful guides for ministers' wives. Most focused on the functional social tasks of a good executive and include chapters such as "Managing Your Household Time."[16] As the basis for proper behavior for a minister's wife, the chapter title cites a publication from the Consumer Education Department of Household Finance Corporation called "Time Management for Home-Makers." The thrust of this genre of literature about clergy families shifts from the more spiritualized, idealized, and passive roles of women in the Roman Catholic Church to the impact of the femininization of American culture. This change was effected through empowerment of service and social organizations, with stress upon the importance of management skills for the pastor's wife as homemaker.

By the time Carolyn P. Blackwood wrote *The Pastor's Wife* in 1951, further shifts were evident in clergy marriage. Blackwood's first chapter, "As a Worthy Woman," depicts the sacramental nature of the minister's wife. Here we find a reemergence of Roman Catholic themes in American homemaking garb: "By fellowship with Christ and by keeping busy, she will soon know how to rise above the level where such things hurt unduly."[17]

Further, in chapter 6, "As a Member of the Flock," Blackwood quotes Ephesians 5:25—"Christ . . . loved the church, and gave himself for it" (KJV), and applies it directly to the minister's wife. This interpretation constitutes a complete role reversal of the woman in the traditional interpretation of this text, where Christ is portrayed as the bridegroom and the church the bride; it was Christ who gave himself for the church. However, in Blackwood's theology, it is the pastor's wife who now takes the place of Jesus! This text probably marks the high watermark in idealizing the minister's wife as the long-suffering, Christlike martyr who, replete with managerial skills and as the power behind the throne, makes everything come together. She is the happy, contented supporter of her husband's work. And she understands her role to be far more material than that of the Blessed Mother, martyr, mystic models of the Roman Catholic Church. The Protestant minister's wife is instead the Andrew Carnegie or the John D. Rockefeller, the pillar of industry who makes the wheels of ministerial functions work for the sake of the kingdom of God.

Shortly after the Blackwood publication appeared, the burgeoning of suburbia and the series of social criticisms of the American harmonious family as epitomized in *The Man in the Gray Flannel Suit* and *Peyton Place* suggested that the American family, including the parsonage family, was far less homogeneous or harmonious than Blackwood assumed. The simple sociological and ecclesial functions and tasks appropriate for pastors' spouses and clergy marriages became suddenly and dramatically more complex.

Our study is an effort first to appreciate the historical development of the priest, nun, and clergy family from biblical times through the 1950s. But our goal is to present an accurate description of the parsonage family today. In our discussion we hope to achieve a clear and realistic view of clergy marriages and the way they will look in the future.

The Early Modern Minister's Family

In this early era of clergy marriages we find unambiguous, stylized roles and behavioral expectations. The early portrait is of a clergy family in which the minister is male, the spouse is a faithful Christian homemaker who reflects the virtues of the Virgin Mary, works with the spiritual industriousness of the mystics, and is willing to martyr herself on behalf of her pastor-husband and "his" church.

This setting captures the image of a slow-moving, stable, homogeneous culture and family life as well as the stark contrast between church and world. The clergy family is a model for ministry that is distinguished from other church members or the larger secular society. In this setting marriages work best when roles are clearly defined, and life exists in the quintessential setting of the small, stable hamlet or village, the county seat town, or the single large downtown church in a larger city setting. And inherent in the portrait are spiritually generic smiles made homogeneous by pose and practice.

The writings of Blackwood, Denton, Fisher, and Haines[18] reinforce the stories related by Margaret Watt. In these clergy family settings, one observes a highly stylized posturing by clergy and spouse, highly visible theological orthodoxy, blending in with predictable clergy dress, and affected pastoral mannerisms. In these essays of the minister and the minister's family, one is impressed by an unruffled, spiritually sublime, and socially tranquil countenance. The clergy marriage is a nuclear family, under patriarchal authority, and energized by a martyr/managerial wife whom people know as the power behind the throne.

This style of clergy family life may quickly be dismissed by some. The reader is pastorally reassured by the subtle inter-weaving of social realism and the pastorally affected lifestyle that the pastor's family represents, a hallmark of stability and spiritual power and poise. The stark realism of such a family does not employ the later devices and techniques designed to disguise blemishes or overwhelm with vivid, diverse activities that distract from obvious flaws. The beauty, serenity, and integrity of the nineteenth- and early twentieth-century clergy family life are compelling.

In this era the proper theological pose and the correct social posture of the good Christian family are difficult to maintain without "blinking." Occasionally a family member is captured with theological eyes averted from the high calling or attention diverted from the stylized family roles and distracted by secular motifs. In these marital settings, many clergy families live socially and maritally frozen in a permanent clergy pose. History forgives little, and diverted, tired, or distracted clergy are obvious. However stylized a clergy family may seem from this background or era, one is inspired by the dedication, wisdom, and generally unquestioned acceptance of the partnership notion of ministerial vocation.

Referral and Determent of Family Tasks. In an era of clergy specialization, some of the tasks gladly accepted by a more traditional family structure are referred outside the clergy home because they are seen as too complicated or specialized to be homebound tasks. Ministers are sent away for seminary training;

the children go away for prep or college education. Many family concerns that traditionally had been part of the minister's family responsiblilities are delegated to others. This shift from home to external agency—whether for entertainment or child daycare— is a net loss in time, quality of life, and money. The benefits that might at first be expected frequently do not occur at the same level or accomplishment as anticipated. For example, the lack of discreet professional advancement by clergy who have earned the D.Min. degree illustrates some of the questionable benefits of achieving a new or higher social and theological status.

By relying on external agencies to perform more and more of the tasks historically associated with the clergy family, the pastor, church, and family have a less focused sense of the unique values and contributions of being a pastor and living in a pastor's family.

The Clergy as Independent Artisans

New Foundations. In this setting, the role of the pastor's wife is much more ambiguous than the long-suffering homemaker who is content to employ skills of nurture, grace, and organization at home. We detect developments here that on the surface seem positive but that may have been achieved at some cost. Here increased cultural opportunities are available to clergy spouses; the ministerial family is more liberated and enters a cultural land of plenty. The pastor's family lives more comfortably with cultural hues that are freer, more colorful, and more subtle than the stark black-and-white contrasts may suggest in previous eras. Social freedoms imply an intimacy and satisfaction that may be a cover-up for estrangement, alienation, and loneliness. Clearly many direct benefits are evident: salary increases, fringe benefits, church-provided housing, automobile allowance, vacation time, and continuing education opportunities.

Cultural Acceptance and Assimilation. As clergy are seen to be more the professional craftsmen than moral and cultural role models, we see typically a greater possibility for cultural inclusiveness for the family. More general cultural benefits are available for the clergy, but life as a "clergy family" is less distinct. The minister's family becomes more colorful, individualized, and less stylized. The positive value of education for clergy and family members is recognized. Development of multiple roles of husband, wife, and children—and the benefits that those bring—combine to enhance clergy-family life.

Little details mean a great deal. In the more traditional setting, clergy families were required to abide by a highly confining clergy stereotype. As American culture expanded after World War II and provided more opportunities, the clergy family came to expect and demand the right to participate in the benefits of the culture at large. More days off, less conservative clothing, flashier cars, and private-line telephones are assumed to be part of the benefit package in this picture. Greater exposure to a public life introduces its own consequence. Small details of life suddenly become magnified and exposed to general public scrutiny, and some of the cultural gains may not contribute to the spiritual or vocational quality of life for the family.

We see additional details of clergy family life as more activities become available for the family. In the tradition-oriented pastor's life, the pastor or family typed, duplicated, and passed out the Sunday church bulletins. Where the pastor is the independent artisan the minister's family becomes incidental to his daily activities. The pastor is now armed with an office, a secretary, and an appointment calendar. Rituals of the clerical office become more stylized for weddings and funerals. Even the Sunday morning worship service becomes more highly structured and liturgical. But the purpose of ministry may get lost. For example, congregations are becoming more impatient with pastors whose Sunday morning services go over sixty minutes. Laity offer a number of reasons: reservations at a local restaurant, the broadcast time of sporting events early in the afternoon, or other time-bound appointments. These expectations press for the pastor as artisan to have rituals of the office of pastor neatly under control. Advantages in technology and specialized skills may be wonderful at the functional level, but efficiency may take over ministerial chores—to the pastor's peril.

In studying this development, one must examine more critically the call to ministry. Is the image of the pastor's wife one solely that of homemaker and manager behind the scenes? How are the "preacher's kids" to work through their adolescent rebellion without bringing public shame to the congregation or scandal to the community? With the increase of clergy independent from the older perfect-example exemplar model, a different set of conflicts will erupt between the clergy family and congregational expectations of them.

For personal gain, clergy may exploit the triangle of pastor–family—congregation. The implicit trust between the pastor's family and the congregation that was true in the more traditional models is not so easily and abundantly offered in this model. Embezzlement of church funds and the fiscal and sexual exploits that came to light in the Jim Bakker and Jimmy Swaggart scandals are serious flaws that threaten to destroy the spiritual integrity of the ministry. What the artisan pastor may stubbornly claim as his private business in marriage, sex, and money may suddenly burst open as public business. The transition from a simple, homogeneous ministerial lifestyle to a more open, adventuresome life suggests that ministry still occurs twenty-four hours a day and never finally is private or independent of a congregation's expectations.

The clergy marriage is on stage constantly, whether as a predetermined pose or informally captured for public view. Consequently, many ministers and their families have been surprised, angered, and divorced because of the discrepancy in the images they endeavor to project of themselves and the picture the public actually observes of clergy-family activities.

Difficulties in Overspecialization

Ministry Is More Than Numbers. Finally, we glimpse triteness and lack of compassion when ministry becomes too specialized and therefore too detached emotionally and spiritually from the parishioners. A prodigious outpouring of literature and tapes on management skills, human relation skills, counseling, and other motivational tools on professional skills development is available to the pastor. The allure of these highly specialized resources may catch the unwary pastor off guard with the notion that ministry is nothing more than skills technology—a kind of preprogrammed computer that requires only that the minister press the start-and-run button and then step back. The result will be ministry with the touch of a pro.

From a technological perspective such efficiencies simply were not possible earlier.

Many tasks can be done in this third or current era in clergy family history. The promise of improved skills of management, speech, personal motivation, and technical assistance for the pastor in performing ministry is not to be criticized. But acquisition of such skills does not automatically enable the pastor to perform superquality ministry.

Ministry Is Not Video Tape. In a high-tech society, a frequent moral illusion is fostered. We come to believe that life is managed by a computer keyboard delete key. We can make bad things go away. Or if a problem exists, the pastor as technician can engage the instant-replay button to reverse a bad decision. We may believe that everything can be done over again without suffering any permanent negative consequence. We agonize in slow-action analysis and use reverse angles to solve problems of judgment and procedure. In the entertainment and news industry the technique may be beneficial, but it is not available for ministry or for the minister's family.

When Automatic Rituals Fail. The wonderful features of highly refined specialty skills in ministry instantly change to serious emergencies when the power behind professional rituals fails. The minister has to know how to take over manually when automatic rituals don't cover a particular problem. Not only do tasks fail, new problems break out spontaneously. For example, many ministers are now in dual-career marriages, with children who are highly active and successful in a variety of activities in church, school, and community. These families may put their lives on automatic pilot and depend on the auto-focus rituals of ministerial office to do an effective job in the daily routines of ministry and home life. But when a child's sudden sickness or another emergency ruins an important professional, social, or civic appearance, pastors and families complain of the stress of living in an auto-focused world in which ministry and family seem lost in the big blurred picture. The value of the automatic or specialized functions for marriage and ministry is the reduction of personal risk or embarrassment by poor-quality performance. The disadvantages lie in the pastor's inability to control the outcome of the whole range of ministerial functions. A "point-and-click" or "automatic-program" mentality for ministry puts the focus always on the general setting or program but not on specific people, issues, uses of time, or personal needs. Such a detached perspective is risky for ministers, however pretty the picture may look initially.

Another problem may rise because the pastor has a ready-made automatic function to blame if ministry and marriage fail to work: my spouse's career had to come first, the church wouldn't adapt to computer-generated mailing lists, the congregation would not respond to my new wardrobe, or the cost-benefit analysis that my CPA provided gave me no choice but to move to greener pastures. Other excuses abound, but psychologically they emanate from a blaming syndrome: if a problem is identified, blame it on someone else or some technological device for not arranging life, marriage, and ministry with clarity and perfect composition.

Venturing a Long Look Down the Road

The diversity of culture, the professionalization of the minister, and the deployment of the minister's family in the work force have been highly celebrated, and the old days of the highly stylized minister and minister's family seem to be fading. But reaction to the yuppie-automated lifestyle is captured by discussions surrounding "mommy track," "daddy track," and getting off the fast track (auto-pilot careers) and returning to traditional family and spiritual values. In the same way that black-and-white photography and its art form are making a comeback in movies, commercials, and personal life, one notices quickly its compelling simplicity in contrast to the auto-focus 35mm cameras and camcords, and explosive MTV-type of overwhelming color and sound. At the same time, we are seeing a renewal of the valuing of chastity and monogamy that to some may seem stark in their contrast to the glitz, glory, color, and pace of a cultural fast lane. Not all ministry will be performed in the future as though in a simple, small-town setting, and specialization and highly technical training will continue to have their place. But bigger, faster, more technical and specialized tasks are not the only way to go in ministry. Though in a very conflicted and complex society, old-fashioned ministry is making a comeback.

Some Advances Here To Stay. In the egalitarian marriage with dual career spouses, the minister's spouse, whether wife or husband, who works outside the home, is a permanent part of ministerial families. When such a lifestyle is running efficiently, it is good. When it breaks down, it is awful because no back-up system, no day-by-day support structure or family member is available to take over manually. The pace is so fast and automatic that family and church responsibilities suddenly go unmet. There is no guaranteed way to take over and make a fast-paced life go smoothly.

New Horizons. The benefits of ministry and appreciation for the variegated textures of ministry will come into sharper focus. Those entering ministry will have a clearer idea of what pastoring requires. Those choosing to stay will know more fully why they are in ministry and will be more informed about the ways their ministry is appreciated by others. Likewise, the local church will have a more realistic idea, a three-dimensional one perhaps, of what cooperative clergy-laity relations should be for the entire congregation. One can anticipate an increase in laity activism to be a part of the future picture of ministry.

Ministry, too, is subject to technological enhancements— whether of speech, electronic and video tape libraries, or from belonging to a "school" of a popular preacher or minister. They are all tempting but few pastors will materially benefit from these high-end technologies, even though many will dabble. Predictably, pastors who become too cute and gimmicky will be seen for who they are. The latest in personal, professional, or office technology will always be tempting. But the latest fad or device will not form a ministry. Only God and the yielding pastor can accomplish that goal.

Conclusion

We have used several metaphors to examine different clergy-family settings and as a means of grouping ministerial family poses and lifestyles. Whether a pastor lives in a traditional setting or moves with the theological fast track of video and audio sermon tapes, computers or FAX machines, one must remember that the clergy family and ministry have to do with the life of the church and not technology. However technically sophisticated we become, we have to remember that the Sacraments abide. The simple elements of bread and wine of the Lord's Supper and the water of baptism remind us that the most profound elements of the faith are the simple things. And so we have faith, hope, and love. But love for God and neighbor, ourselves, and the church is the adhesive that holds us together in ministry—if we understand that we love because God loved us first. Ultimately, love—God's love for us, and the pastor's for ministry and family—is the force that binds the various historical portraits of ministry in a cohesive manner.

2

Theological Call

The call to serve Christ and his church is a charge all Christians accept to one degree or another. One may view it as a way in which he/she should conduct all of life, or, at least, a way to bring up his/her children. It may be viewed as God's beckoning to the vocation of ministry, perhaps a challenge to enter the mission field. Or serving Christ may mean exploring one's strengths to determine what one can offer the world, rather than the church, *per se*, in the name of Christianity.

Spiritual growth and calling are as gradual to some as physical growth. Though one cannot look into the mirror one morning and see actual change taking place, growth is evident nonetheless. A female Episcopal priest saw that being called is

> . . . like falling in love with that very special person. It comes to each person in a different way. God, Love itself, has an incredible capacity to touch each particular personality where it is most vulnerable to His love. To some, a Paul, it comes like a thunderbolt of recognition; to another, a Peter, like a gentle beckoning of conviction; to another, a Joseph of Arimathaea, a painful growth of spiritual awareness. Yet, in every case, one is never the same again. One's life takes on a dimension of trust and confidence inconceivable before.[1]

Perhaps some are more eager to see tangible and unambiguous evidence of spiritual calling, while to others it may be that there is the unexplainable yet inescapable call to drop one's net and follow (Mt. 4:18–20).

29

The common bond shared by all Christians is belief in God and the work of the Lord in our lives. Each person experiences God's call in a unique way. To some, the call originates from the soul—as a distinct yearning or pull toward full-time Christian service. For others friends, teachers, or family members have recognized a particular gift for the ministry. Through the voice of a youth director, Sunday school teacher, or church member others are encouraged to delve more actively into the possibility of ministry as a vocation. The strength of a call may be seen in the certainty with which one's own vocation is directed toward Christian ministry. For others it is confirmed in the deep, spiritual awareness that God will take care of us as we surrender our lives in Christian service. The assurance that one's personal life as well as family are in good hands, when one is called into ministry, is expressed by a Church of the Nazarene minister:

> When we are called of God, the Lord will take care of us and our families. If it is our choosing an occupation, there could be problems.

This pastor's dedication to Christian ministry is reinforced by a theological self-confidence by which he and his family "know" that God will provide and care for them, if they but follow the Abrahamic call into ministry.

No call to ministry is so simple and easy as to exist without conflict. Stress within and pressures without may in fact increase. Those truly called understand the conflicts of the Abrahamic call and live their vocation faithfully in spite of pressures. An Assemblies of God pastor sums it up:

> A lot of pressures are involved with the ministry. But I believe it is the most important job in the world. I also feel that God called me. I would not be happy doing anything else.

This sense of calling, bonding, and connectedness with God, ministry in the church, and the firm confidence that God will provide what is necessary for the family are clearly expressed by these two pastors. To elaborate on a theological concept of vocation as calling and to convey the mystery that comes with the call, one may liken the various dimensions of a spiritual calling to the variety of possible telephone hookups. Who is it? What does God want to say to me? Why is God calling me? Distance and some awkwardness always exist between the caller and the called, but the vocation of ministry is the contact that unites God and pastor.

Regardless of the mechanism or device that connects God to pastor, the message is clear to those who receive the call. One is being called to serve God. One may hear a good deal of "ringing," "whistles and bells," that some others also acknowledge as part of their experience of the call. However, the call also may be a quiet, nearly profound silence out of which God speaks. One cannot prove by visible or tangible means that he/she has been called. Yet in faith one answers. Being called into the ministry is a faith venture that carries with it many theological, personal, and denominational implications.

Not all are called to the same type of ministry: "God has appointed in the church first apostles, second prophets, third teachers, then workers of miracles, then healers, helpers, administrators, speakers in various kinds of tongues" (1 Cor. 12:28).

Many different types of ministries or levels of ministry exist as an expression of one's call. John Calvin wrote, ". . . in order that noisy and troublesome men should not rashly take upon themselves to teach or to rule (which might otherwise happen), especial care was taken that no one should assume public office in the church without being called. Therefore, if a man were to be considered a true minister of the church, he must first have been duly called (Heb. 5:4), then he must respond to his calling, that is, he must undertake and carry out the task enjoined."[2]

No one claims that it is easy to respond to God's call. Whether one has been trying from birth to fulfill or understand God's call or has been dramatically called to drop the fishing nets of an established occuptation, many dreams may have to be set aside if one is to follow the call. In the biblical account of Jesus' call of Peter and Andrew, Jesus declares that he will make them "fishers of men." The message for the pastor in this paradigm is that when he or she responds to the call and becomes a fisher of people, God promises to use the skills, interests, talents, dedication—even frustrations and heartbreaks—that the called one already had as a fisher of fishes. To be a minister is not to live the easy life. In many ways it is a more difficult life because it is complicated by the fact that the minister has responsibilities not for getting a net full of fish to shore but a congregation full of souls into safe harbor. An Assemblies of God pastor writes:

Overall, the stress and problems would be the same or about the same whether I am a minister or not. How I handle things is what makes the difference. The one major difference in my work is my life; there's no leaving it at the office, but this is why a calling is a must.

The implication of this pastor's observation about both the difficulties and the joys of being a pastor is that without God's help the task would be impossible. One is on call twenty-four hours a day. The tasks never stop at the end of a nine-to-five time frame, and the responsibilities of caring for souls is ever present. Therefore, as this pastor suggests, unless one has a firmly entrenched, confident sense of call, ministry will quickly become frustrating, stressful, and destructive to pastor and family.

Eloquent testimony to the necessity of reassurance of a call is expressed by a Christian Church (Disciples) clergy:

A pastor will incur more problems and yield to stress when he/she and the spouse are doing ministry outside of a personal relationship with Jesus and outside the call from God. Many seminary classmates had no call, denied such existed, and treated the role of the pastor as an occupation.

Whether one is a fisherman, computer operator, nurse, teacher, successful entrepreneur, often becoming a clergy means giving up a profession that has required extensive effort, financial outlay, apprenticeship, and for many the beginnings of achievement and recognition in the secular job. For those who have tasted success in a non-ministerial role, the requirement to go to seminary requires far more sacrifice than a change of secular jobs or adjustment to a lower income. They must become knowledgeable in fields of history, humanities, and English, which may be too dissimilar from one's background in science, math, or physics. Ministry requires an entirely new orientation to life. This is putting the nets of life down on the other side of the ship.

Others may find that years of fumbling and stumbling, of living in quiet unhappiness are ended and they find peace in finally answering the "oppressive call" into Christian ministry. We are promised more than is conceivable if we take on the role and responsibility of serving God in response to Christ's call.

But it is not without cost and a great deal of effort in our lives, work, and hearts—and to our families.

Whatever one's situation with respect to the call, God's beckoning into ministry is never a guarantee of an easy personal transition, nor does it make the minister's family life simply divine. A United Methodist minister put it:

> I love being what I am. I am called by God. There are times I would give it all up for a nickel but I can't.

An American Baptist clergy said:

> God called me to the ministry, and I did not pick it as a means of a living. This in itself is at times a problem for the children to understand. Many things other kids in the area have they cannot . . . they are too costly and unaffordable.

One's spiritual and emotional security are put to the test in the call to ministry. One may have to work harder at resolving difficulties, whether financial, emotional, spiritual, or family-related. The more open and eager one is to accept the challenge and call into ministry, the more apt one is to work out the problems and/or obstacles encountered along the way, especially family needs and expectations.

Direct Connection With God

Being deeply attuned to God's call may be like dialing a toll-free number. The connection is instantaneous, clear, and without static or conflict. It will require the rest of one's life to assimilate and live out consequences of the conversation. But the deep, nearly effortless spiritual connection with God comes to those who, having heard God's call, respond without hesitation to God's beckoning into Christian service.

A focused sense of call is fulfilling to the clergy, his/her family, and the congregation. Across the board, comments from respondents show that the most fulfilled, contented, satisfied ministers at home and in the church are those who look upon the call to ministry as a spiritual, vocational summons and not as a profession. Even then problems may be encountered. A Church of God, Anderson, pastor finds:

My whole life and family are centered around the church. Criticism is sometimes hard to take when you are wholeheartedly serving the Lord.

The implications of this pastor's self-assessment is that despite the clarity of one's spiritual call, pastors need assurance of support from spouse and children if ministry is to be deeply satisfying.

A similar positive expression comes from a Presbyterian Church in America clergy:

Overall, I can join the apostle Paul and say, "Woe is me if I preach not the gospel." I find that pressures on the family come with the calling. What counts is how a pastor deals with those pressures.

The happiest and most fulfilled in their call are undeniably those who do not limit their ministry or call to the confines of the church or a nine-to-five schedule. These clergy integrate their calling into their very existence. Being called is not viewed as an affliction but as a way of life or opportunity for unlimited spiritual fulfillment. Glen E. Whitlock maintains, "The office of the ordained minister is properly placed within the context of Christian vocation. It is not an office that sets a man apart in terms of status. It sets him apart only in functional or operational terms. 'Operational' is derived from operari, 'to work.' It is the special work of ministry to which a person is called. He is called to stand in the place where he can serve."[3] The families of these ministers are happy, and with good reason; the minister is fulfilled. The obstacles and stresses that come with ministry are viewed as a challenge instead of an inconvenience, and the family shares in the secure, sound theological foundation that has been set at home as well as in the clergy's workplace. The sense of vocation is not broken by interruption or disturbed family time. When the family is together, they enjoy their devotion to each other, conversation, and Christian fellowship. The family is less concerned about the time away because it is seen as an integral part of the whole of the clergy's dedication to Christian life and ministry. It is important at this point to affirm that clergy do need to claim time for family and take time to be with family.

Making the Call Clear

Formal Education. Educational requirements can have either a positive or negative effect on the way in which ministers view their vocation. Data from our survey indicate that denominations requiring the most extensive formal training have clergy who view ministry not as a vocation but as a profession. The time, money, and effort expended in meeting educational requirements of the denomination somehow cause ministers to think that that is what they had to put into it. Now the question concerns what they can get out of it. When ministry is seen as a profession versus a vocation, many complications ensue. The drive to maintain upward mobility and receive benefits befitting a "professional" can result in great frustration for some. A PCUSA minister commented:

> Even so-called well-paid pastors are not paid well by [current] professional standards. Pastors are professionals with graduate degrees and should be paid to hire outside help in the homefront in order to entertain. Pay is my biggest criticism.

While pay may be a realistic criticism, certainly in ministry as well as in all of life money can't solve every problem. If this pastor is not careful, a doubling of salary would probably not preclude the same criticism from being leveled at the church. For ministers a negative comparison with other professionals is self-defeating. There will always be other ministers, attorneys, physicians, and even those without graduate or professional degrees who will make many times the number of dollars of a pastor. Being a "well-paid pastor" can at best be only a relative statement. Ministry is a vocation that begins at the Cross and not at a bankteller's window.

Ministry, like all other vocations, is not always static-free. Many hours of frustrating, emotionally unfulfilling, physically draining, and spiritually bewildering tasks and obligations are inherent. The complaint by a Christian Church (Disciples) pastor implies that his focus is on the static and frustration, not the calling itself:

> My first ten years in the ministry were very frustrating. I was far more educated than those with whom I worked and not very stimulated by them. I simply wasn't challenged as a minister. It

was a pretty routine profession. Frustration took its toll on me and my family.

One United Methodist pastor reflects in his complaint the educational naïveté of some ministers who believe in a high, positive correlation between formal education, income, and job satisfaction:

> . . . it doesn't make any sense to have this educational background for a profession that can't meet the needs of my family.

The ministry is not the road to take for financial security, though its spiritual and emotional benefits far outweigh the financial gains sought. Yet bills still have to be paid, and one may have only limited time away from the church for vacation.

This fact is not to argue that the pastor should not want the best for his/her family. Nor is desire for success, rcognition, and promotion wrong. Far from it! Acceptance of a call by God to the ministry is done in faith. Before accepting a call, it is wise for a pastor to consider and discuss with the family financial limitations and mobility factors. Christ urges us to consider the cost of construction before beginning to build, and that principle applies here. Such a discussion should include the restraints, opportunities, and frustrations of ministry. To the best of one's spiritual and emotional ability, and with family considerations in mind, one needs to count the cost of Christ's calling, "the cost of discipleship," at the beginning stages of a call. Acceptance of God's call will bring its own rewards in this life as well as those spiritual rewards that may not not be realized on earth but in heaven. There can and will be limitations and these should be considered as inherent in the call to ministry.

Informal Education. One's background in the church and any imbibing of theological and spiritual issues will be either positively or negatively influential as he/she considers God's call. If, for example, the one called or the spouse is a PK (preacher's kid), that person will cope more successfully with the issues involved. An Assemblies of God pastor wrote:

> Since my wife was a PK, she had a good grasp of what the ministry would be like. She also understands the interruptions that the ministry can bring to family life. If she were not familiar with those aspects of ministry, my job would be much more difficult.

One might consider this kind of family relationship as a kind of a spiritual conference call. Both the pastor and his wife are tuned in to the same spiritual conversation, and he affirms the strength this gives him and the family. Here the pastor clearly feels called, and the spouse's background enables her to understands what that call involves.

A comparable testimony is offered by another pastor:

> Living with parents who were in the ministry gave me a desire to follow in their footsteps. Although they faced hard challenges during those years, they never complained or showed bitterness to us or others.

The sense of responsibility, public exposure, private fulfillment, and obligation is expressed eloquently by an Episcopal priest:

> Because my father was a priest I was well aware of some of the problems involved in clergy families. I have avoided many of those because of that fact. Also, I was aware of some of the perceptions that people often have concerning the minister, his job, and his family. Being a role model does not bother me; if it did, I wouldn't be here.

Despite the bad press that PKs receive from some, another Episcopal priest reflects the early sense of calling and of being tuned in to his father's spiritual call and its positive impact on his own life:

> I was a child of a clergyman and was very happy during the time I was under my parents' roof. I know that I would not be happy doing anything else than being a priest in God's holy catholic church.

The social and family background of the pastor's spouse is important as far as frank discussions on the issues involved in a call are concerned. Affirming the ease of communication both horizontally between this Lutheran pastor and his wife and the vertical conversation between him and his wife and God is seen in his affirming comments:

> I was a pastor before my wife and I met. Her father's vocation was good preparation for her. She was aware of demands on time and of being on call twenty-four hours. Also, she was aware of how difficult people can be when they are conflictual.

All of these influences contribute to the way in which one formulates ideas and perceptions of the church and the ministry.

The Church As Family. In a positive church experience, a minister and his/her family feel the support and encouragement of the congregation. The pastor feels close to the congregation and finds assistance in working out the sense of call. The spouse and children may find that they are adopted by the congregation and therefore have a large extended family. This experience is very positive and fulfilling for the minister, his/her spouse, the children, and the congregation.

As in all healthy families, even the best match of clergy and congregation may have problems. Dealing with problems in the church can bring the minister and congregation closer together just as confronting and dealing with family problems can strengthen the family unit. Many ministers find their sense of call strengthened and reaffirmed time and again by confronting in a positive way any issues and problems that rise in the life of the church. In a real sense, for good or ill, the congregation becomes family for the clergy family. Where an openness of relationship, communication, and mutual calling exists, the experience is positive. Consider the testimony of two American Baptist ministers:

> At its best the local church serves as an extended faith family for us. Being removed from grandma and grandpa, the intergenerational dimensions of the local church help to fill family needs for extended nurture, moral, and value building.

> The kids have enjoyed the care and love shown them by many of the older members. It has almost been like having eight or nine sets of grandparents. They enjoy that part of church life very much.

A United Methodist minister is equally affirming of the extended family concept of his congregation:

> We have taken members of the congregation as extra family. We are enriched with children, grandparents, sisters, and brothers of different races and socio-economic statuses.

For those who long for the congregation to become a family member to substitute for parents with whom one may be in conflict, an Episcopal clergy warns:

The church makes a lousy mother. Any minister expecting "mom" to take care of him/her will be sadly disappointed.

Putting the issue properly in perspective, a Lutheran minister underscores the value of the supportive role of the congregation for the minister without one's expecting the congregation to be a substitute mom or dad:

> We have a strong common faith, which helps us through the stresses. The congregation is very supportive and understanding and treats the family as any other. We all have many close friends in the congregation.

Peer Group. The minister may find encouragement from other clergy who deal with stresses and issues similar to one's own. Opportunity to share the joys and burdens of a call to ministry with someone who understands and has been through similar experiences is of great benefit to pastors, their families, and their respective congregations. A PCUSA minister commented:

> The group for newly ordained pastors in my presbytery offered me a wonderful opportunity to share with other new ministers the ups and downs of serving a church. Without this support group I would have been unable to see that I am not the only one facing these challenges.

A female United Church of Christ pastor states:

> The church community provides much support and love although they are not our close friends. I also feel isolated because there are few married clergy women with families with whom I can compare notes.

And a Lutheran minister commented:

> Being a pastor tends to isolate me and my family from the remainder of the congregation. Added to this I have found that rarely do we as pastors seek to associate at too personal a level with other pastors. The ordained ministry can be very lonely for pastors and his/her family.

The lack of a support group was acutely felt by one American Baptist pastor who stated:

> There is no couple that we can treat as confidential friends because of the confusion of personal and professional roles. . . . There is no one with whom we can share our excitement/concern/frustration.

Providing a structure in which pastors can support each other in their own denominations should be available to all ministers, and should be a priority for denominational officials.

Connection/Wrong Call

All of us have had the experience of being both embarrassed and at times irritated by misdialing a number and either waking someone rudely in the middle of the night or having someone let us know in no uncertain terms that we reached the wrong number. The concept of a wrong number suggests that people who try to dial God on their own terms may instead either hear a permanent busy tone or reach the wrong party. The call into ministry originates with God and is not the result of our success in dialing. Vocational wrong numbers and bad connections are occasionally reached in several ways.

Floundering Life. Some individuals may think ministry is a safe or convenient place to resolve problems of a confused life. This constitutes more of a forced or self-imposed call than a true call from God. The result of an individual taking on the responsibility of ministry without a true call can be disastrous both for the clergy and his/her family and for the congregation.

No Safe Harbor. The ministry is not a safe place for weary travelers to hide. Misconceptions and problems that the unhappy or discontented pastor brings into the ministry simply escalate both for the pastor and the unwitting congregation. The ministry is not a place for people to "park" or "tie up" to avoid the storms of life.

Not only in parish settings do we see pastors dialing the wrong number by trying to force themselves into a safe harbor of personal tranquility that does not exist. A community of eager ministers-to-be is a great place to feel at home and obtain unconditional acceptance that is not always readily available in educational or professional environments. A warning sign of this vocational bad connection occurs when the pastor spends a disproportionate amount of time in professional peer-group settings, retreats, leadership roles, or can never be found accountable in day-by-day parish or congregational tasks. Where this happens the pastor is simply trying to float around a safe harbor away from the storms of life and drawing a sense of security from whomever: fellow pastors, individuals in the congregation, from hobbies, excessive sermon preparation and library usage, trivialized social concern activities, or excessive amounts of "being present" in a passive way in any number of activities.

In seminary settings one often sees the walking wounded, individuals unable to find a vocational niche where they feel comfortable. What better place to find nurturing and unspoken acceptance than in an environment surrounded by ministers-to-be? The seminary environment can be a nurturing, supportive place. On the other hand, at one seminary a ministerial student, blind from birth, was helped by fellow students in every aspect of daily life. Someone laid out his clothes every morning, another carried his tray at mealtime, another helped with his class work, and someone walked him across the streets. Students felt good helping; after all, he was blind and seminary was a fostering, Christian community. But when the blind student completed his seminary education, he left more dependent on people than he was when he arrived four years earlier. This "fostering, nurturing" community had rendered him more dependent and less able to face the real world. Fortunately, this is not always the case.

A call to the ministry is an important and great work that is to be entered upon only after careful reflection and self-evaluation. Those who choose Godwork out of a desire for a safe place in this world or from a need to be unconditionally accepted in a Christian environment will not succeed in achieving a sense of satisfaction with themselves or from their role as minister. Therefore, it is as important for the prospective minister as it is the seminary professors, candidate committees, and denominational officials to take a long and serious look at the seminary student's intentionality in undertaking the ministry.

The Gunny Sack Ministry. The baggage that one carries into the ministry may prevent fulfillment of his/her sense of call. The vocational gunny sack may hold false assumptions and expectations and unresolved conflicts. All of these have to be overcome before one can be an effective minister. These deceptions and hidden traps may produce a sense of call that is spurious, that is not from God. The person who enters the ministry to have his/her own needs met will be unable effectively to meet the needs of parishioners. At the same time, the pastor may be so deceived about the genuineness of his call that he will not ever recognize that it was not from God. Shouldering the weight of unresolved personal issues added to other conflicts encountered in the ministry can overwhelm even the best technically prepared ministers.

Recognizing and dealing with these gunny-sack issues is the first step toward a more effective ministry. As we imply above, one must consider that this excess baggage may have prompted one to enter the ministry in the first place. Any challenge that one may encounter in the ministry is an opportunity to reevaluate one's sense of call to discover hidden agendas or other unresolved issues. A United Church of Christ pastor laments:

> I am in counseling now, and one of the interesting issues I'm dealing with is what it was like growing up in a minister's family. There were some benefits but even more drawbacks. I have promised myself that I will never have children because I don't want to subject children to the kind of environment I grew up in.

An Episcopal priest reflects upon similar challenges and obstacles in his life:

> Prior to dealing with my codependency issues and addictive behavior, my need to be a fixer led me to a helping profession and was a source of much anguish to me, my family, and parishes. No ministerial candidate should be ordained who has not dealt with these issues, especially as they apply to his family of origin. Unless the candidate has dealt with these issues, the effect may prove to be overwhelming or distract from the family's emotional health.

Negative Professional Comparisons. A sure sign of a wrong number or bad connection is the pastor who continually uses the language, concepts, and behavior patterns of other professions. A wrong vocational identity is on the line if the pastor always talks like a golfer, a financier, a physician, an attorney, a pilot, a farmer, a schoolteacher, or a politician. Under the surface one could expect direct and subtle negative comparisons between the identity, vocation, and opportunities of a minister as contrasted with the over-adulation, positive comparison, and flattering imagery of other professions. But ministers are not politicians, financiers, physicians, attorneys, golfers, pilots, farmers, or retirees. They are called into active ministry and service for the Gospel of Jesus Christ.

Prank Calls

Some use the Lord's work as a smokescreen to hide from or cover over personal gain and manipulation of others. We are not asking pastors to be perfect, but there are those who use ministry as a tool to achieve what they want while fighting what God wants. The concept of a prank call carries the image that the individual placing the call is playing with, manipulating, and abusing the person receiving the call. In this case it's the congregation that lives with the prankster because the telephone lines of Christian vocation are abused.

Abuse of Privileged Communications. Ministers are viewed as chosen by God to carry out divine initiatives. Who can argue with God's representative? Clergy are given a power over people that is unlike power in most other professions. Doctors have the ability to heal, yet they are still seen as capable of human error. Clergy, on the other hand, are presumed to be chosen and directed by God and can misuse their power to gain financial, emotional, and sexual control of others.

The Naïveté of the Call System. Especially difficult for congregations that call their clergy is the establishment of standards and expectations on the part of both parties. If written standards and defined expectations do not result from discussions between the parties, a congregation opens itself to ministerial prank calls. When that occurs, destructive consequences come to the congregation, the clergy, and the clergy family members. It is theologically naïve and in some ways theologically manipulative for a congregation to grant a pastor *carte blanche*, giving no guidance or stated expectations. Pastors need to know of these expectations so that together the parties can determine to make the relationship work. If a good "theological connection" is not established, sooner rather than later the relationship will disconnect.

Successful Connections

Those pastors whose divine call to the ministry is confirmed by the immediate family, the congregation, and the pastor's own sense of certainty of the call are more apt to be in ministry for the long term. We found little difference in this regard among pastors of the eleven denominations we surveyed. Pastors who report a high degree of satisfaction affirm the value of a clear sense of calling and enjoy support from the family and open communication with the congregation. They also develop realistic expectations for themselves and the congregation. The result enhances probability of an effective ministry, a continuing effort to improve their ministry, and the quality of their personal and family life.

The greatest indicator of clergy "success" in the parish is the pastor's ability to affirm, reflect, and build upon a sense of spiritual or theological fulfillment. This pastor will have a positive sense of personal and theological accomplishment and be comfortable with God's call regardless of the size and location of the church, the salary, and his/her marital status. Those who see the ministry as simply another profession are apt to move into negative professional comparisons, adversarial positions with both the congregation and the family, and finally depreciate their abilities in ministry. Without a firm sense of vocational call at the beginning and end of any phase of ministry, the pastor will become dissatisfied, a fact that will adversely affect the family and the congregation.

One way to encapsulate the positive sense of vocation is to recall the words of St. Paul to the church at Philippi: "Have this mind among yourselves, which you have in Christ Jesus, who, though he was in the form of God, did not count equality with God a thing to be grasped, but emptied himself, taking the form of a servant, being born in the likeness of men" (2:5-7).

The mind of Christ resident in the pastor's heart is the greatest guarantee of both pastoral and familial satisfaction and success.

3

Establishing
Correct Priorities

Introduction

The relationship of clergy to their families transcends their relationship to the congregation. One way of depicting this complex relationship is to employ the metaphor of "the tree of ministry." This would include the tree, the soil that supports it, and the root system. One is reminded of Jesus' own metaphorical use of the vine and the branches (John 15:1–11). If the reader will imagine the vitality, complexity, hardship, beauty, and the interdependence of the ecosphere of a forest, one begins to appreciate the complex interaction of the clergy, the clergy family, the extended family of the church, and the relationship of these aspects of a marital ecosphere to the call of God and the kingdom of God.

The dimensions of the delicate spiritual ecological balance of the clergy family and the church are typified in this comment by one Presbyterian pastor:

> It takes a conscious effort to keep my priorities straight, but I shared with the Pastor Search Committee before coming here six years ago that my family is more important to me than the institutional church. I know I am a person before I'm a minister. My wife and children are growing, emotionally healthy persons with good self-esteem who feel fine about my work.

This pastor has identified the life of his ministry as a flourishing plant because he places his family above the institutional church. If he loses his hold on his family in doing ministry, pastoring will lose its spiritual significance as far as he is concerned. His ministry will have been overpowered by the institutional church. For this pastor neither his family nor his congregation can enjoy healthy spiritual self-esteem unless his family's value is preserved. The family in this example is a spiritual bellwether of the congregation's spiritual and emotional health. If the pastor's family suffers, the institution is already not well.

For other pastors, the priorities come in different rankings. Our findings suggest that pastors who are able to identify their priorities and negotiate them clearly and directly with the leadership of the congregation enjoy a satisfying pastorate. If priorities are not claimed and acted upon, the pastor, the pastor's family, and the congregation suffer and flounder until they are identified and established. Further, the consequence of those priorities must be understood in the light of their strengths and weaknesses for ministry.

In this chapter, we identify major components by which we analyze the ways that clergy and their families establish priorities and their probable consequences.

Spiritual Rootage

The most significant priority of ministry is development of a deep spiritual rootage for ministry. One is called into a relationship with Jesus Christ, and, through the refiner's fire, into the acceptance, understanding, and experience of being a minister of the Gospel. Family, friends, peers, church members, and supervisors form their assessment of the pastor's effectiveness according to the openness with which he or she identifies the work as a spiritual calling. Continuing conversation between the pastor and significant others refines and clarifies the pastor's calling and establishes the deep spiritual taproot of faith and ministry.

In his discussion about personal salvation and vocation in the church, the author of Hebrews cites King David, Joshua, and other spiritual leaders of the ancient Israel as exemplars of those who "enter into the Lord's rest." This is a deep peace that comes from knowing that one is doing God's will. In Hebrews 4:13 we have the compelling image of the Word of God as a two-edged sword that cuts away everything but the taproot of our existence: "Before [God] no creature is hidden, but all are open and laid bare to the eyes of him with whom we have to do." The image of being laid bare reminds us that only a full surrender, without spiritual or psychological pretense, clears the way for the taproot of spiritual maturity to flourish.

The teaching of Hebrews 4 is a call to develop ministerial taproots for today's pastor and calls him or her to be spiritually "open and laid bare." The more spiritually vulnerable one becomes, the deeper will be the Christian taproot that produces the growth, strength, and increased capacity to endure in the Gospel. If one's spiritual life is deep in the soil of the Gospel, one's sense of vocation will endure. Each individual pastor must clarify in his or her own time and experience what that taproot is and which hidden and guarded aspects of life must be surrendered to God for ministry's sake. In releasing pretense and superficial satisfactions, the pastor achieves a deep, resilient commitment.

Accompanying the clarity of spirituality is a greater capacity for growth, ministry, constancy, and resolve between the clergy and the family. The powerful forces that drive one toward willingness to be open and laid bare to the Gospel may originate in a deep sense of a personal encounter with Jesus Christ. Or those forces may be the sensitive and compassionate nurturing of a pastor years before or from the current congregation. Or they may come on wings of a family crisis. Or be a gradual awakening to unaddressed social ills. These powerful spiritual forces may come as an uneasy awareness that one's present lifestyle, goals, and peer group's activities are truly a waste of time and a prostitution of one's gifts. Whatever the source or avenue of vocational conviction, it is obvious in our study that the deeper the spiritual taproot and rootage of ministry the clearer the focus of one's vocation.

The taproot of ministerial vocation is a matter of Christian faith. Our survey results clearly suggest that many take the initial step toward a calling. But few complete the arduous tasks required to enter the active pastoral ministry. Being chosen is more than personal preference. Ministry is a choosing that comes from God's activity, and is a choosing to be embraced by each individual pastor. Some are able to effect this choosing/chosenness in a brief period of time. Others may require twenty or thirty years of ministry to confirm it and reconcile themselves to it. Others have never been able to effect the deep rootage of choosing/chosen regardless of the faith language employed before a congregation, on an application form, or in a written theological statement.

We repeat an Episcopal clergyman's comments on this deep, profound sense of choosing/chosen:

> I was a child of a clergyman and was very happy under my parents' roof. I know that I would not be happy doing anything other than being a priest in God's holy catholic church. My children were never forced to attend church, but they knew they were expected to. They are now on their own, and do attend Episcopal churches.

Here the taproot clearly passes through the deep fertile soil of three generations of dedicated, satisfied church families. The certitude, clarity, and resolve are self-evident in this priest's reflection about his sense of satisfaction in ministry and his family's.

An American Baptist pastor reflects with a wry expression of satisfaction and slight embarrassment a similar sense of the spiritual depth and taproot security offered in Hebrews 4:

> We are a young, attractive couple with a lifestyle of two old fudds. We are fulfilled by what we do, but live for vacation time when we can meet our needs with lots of rest and relaxation.

We can conclude that whatever happens personally and within the family this pastor has come to terms with his vocation as seen in his phrase "a lifestyle of two old fudds." His may be a self-depreciating statement, but it reflects the power flowing from a deep spiritual taproot that is not confused with superficial evidences of satisfaction and dissatisfaction.

A Lutheran pastor expresses the personal sense of frustration about achieving his deep spiritual taproot:

> Dr. Bill Lazereth said once, "When I'm a good pastor, I'm not a good husband and father, when I am a good husband, I'm not a good pastor and father, and when I'm a good father, I'm not a good pastor or husband." It might be extreme, but I feel it's a good way to put what the stress on ministers in the twentieth century is. I try to live out a balance between pastor, husband, and father.

Establishing and extending the spiritual taproot is never easy for any pastor.

We recall the different perspective an Assemblies of God pastor took as he reflected positively on the spiritual rootage of his life and marriage:

> Since my wife was [a pastor's daughter], she had a good grasp of what the ministry would be like. She also understands the interruptions that the ministry can bring to family life. If she were not familiar with those aspects of ministry, my job would be much more difficult. An understanding and supportive spouse is essential to effective ministry, at least in a small community.

One might observe that regardless of community size, congregation, or length of ministry, "an understanding and supportive spouse is essential to effective ministry."

The Pastor's Personality Makeup

We have identified four aspects of a pastor's personality that are indicators of a stable basis for ministry functions and those personal dimensions of one's life that are most readily cited as strengths and weaknesses for effective ministry.

Interrelationship of Occupation and Personality. Several studies since the 1940s have examined the relationship between occupation and personality. They suggest that no clear-cut personality variable can predict job success.[1] The debate is unresolved as to whether particular personalities are attracted to specific occupations because of psychological makeup or whether certain occupations attract personalities because of the psychological traits that work well in those occupations. Concerning clergy, the dominant trait needed for successful ministry and that is valued in personality is the tendency to nurture. Therefore, as we might expect, most clergy rank high on nurturing scales.

The Minnesota Multiphasic Personality Inventory (MMPI) is a test that was designed in the early 1940s and has a high reliability factor. Of numerous MMPI profiles available to us,[2] clergy score high on the nurturing scale. This is indicated by the elevated scores on the Mf scale for the MMPI. Originally indicated as a masculine/feminine scale, it is more accurate to consider this as a social sensitivity or nurturing indicator. High scores on this variable indicate a profile of an individual who has well developed social and personal sensitivities that stress expressive functions such as speech, group discussion, music, emotional crises, etc. High Mf scores suggest a sensitivity that can easily be developed toward increased social sensitivities.

Among ministers we would anticipate good teaching skills, good pastoral care sensibilities, an appreciation for public speaking, music, and a social awareness of both emotional and social needs of others. Low scores on the Mf scale would suggest social coarseness, insensitivity to others, lack of sympathy for hurts, pains, and emotional needs of others.

Corresponding to the high capacity to provide nurture and social and personal sensitivity, the typical pastor has high needs for acceptance, affirmation, and nurture. This correlation would be expected.

The first three scales of the MMPI, (Hs)—essentially an optimism/pessimism scale, (D)—essentially a discouragement/self-esteem scale, and (Hy)—a naïve and self-centered/socially isolated and cynical scale are significant profiles. On these three scales, clergy profiles often follow what is known as the "neurotic triad." This pattern is an elevated Hs score, a low D score, and an elevated Hy score. This profile suggests that many clergy have a personal need always to be optimistic. A low D score indicates an active, alert, cheerful demeanor. And the elevated Hy score reveals a naïve, self-centered and narcissistic personality. The combination of these scores creates the neurotic triad, suggesting people with "an extreme need to interpret their problems in a rational and socially acceptable way."[3]

This profile suggests that clergy have a high need to be optimistic and outgoing on the job and in relation to others. They are generally active and function well in the discharge of their social responsibilities. Correspondingly, clergy have a high need to be affirmed and may have difficulty being realistic instead of optimistic about life, marriage, and job. The latter is consequent upon their need always to be optimistic, an indication of social naïveté. They may also have problems establishing long-term plans and strategies for themselves and their churches because of their naïveté and narcissistic need for continual affirmation.

The neurotic triad profile suggests further that clergy refuse to consider more than one way to solve problems because they are more comfortable as nurturers, which would appear to offer a lower risk of conflict. In this pattern, the highly nurturing clergy feel compelled to interpret problems, strategies, and solutions in rational and socially acceptable ways. The inherent inner conflict is obvious, but social conflicts may not surface. The tug-of-war between pastoral and family responsibilities, the need to maintain optimism both at church and at home, and to be cheerful, alert, and pleasing leaders at church and home will create high levels of stress for them. Coupled with the likelihood of their naïveté and self-centeredness about conflict resolution, they place themselves in direct and continuing conflict with their families who have to live with them in their roles of spouses, parents, and spiritual leaders.

Another psychological test familiar to many clergy and their families is the Myers/Briggs Type Indicator (MBTI). This test produces a four-part scale. The first is Extroversion vs. Introversion; the second is Sensing vs. Intuition; third is Thinking vs. Feeling; and the fourth scale is Judging vs. Perceiving. Many clergy fall on the introversion side of the first scale. That does not mean clergy are psychological wallflowers, isolated and withdrawn. It means that their values tend to come from an internal frame of reference. For those who have a strong faith, a thoughtful intellect, and want to think before acting, the introversion scale makes that behavior more possible than does the extroversion scale.

Clergy tend to be about equally divided between whether they think by means of sensing, which is relating to the data immediately available, or its opposite, intuition, which is a form of "possibility thinking." Most strong, intuitive pastors will also be narcissistic and somewhat naïve in their efforts to make all possibilities come true. Sensing pastors will be more plodding but realistic about achievable goals. Further, most pastors fall in the Feeling side of the scale, the opposite of Thinking. This profile is correlated with the high MMPI scale on nurture. The Myers/Briggs Thinking type means that the individual assesses a problem, draws intellectual conclusions, and acts on them while maintaining relatively low sensitivity to the emotional impact or consequence on others. One who operates by a feeling mode is concerned about the feelings and reactions of individuals and groups.

Finally, the majority of pastors fall into the Perceiving category. This category, along with their nurturing gifts, means clergy perceive very well the issues that are presented as pastoral concerns, social concerns, preaching, or teaching concerns. However, these pastors have difficulty coming to closure or exercise action judgments toward identified goals. Judgment, in this sense, refers to drawing a conclusion, making an assessment, and acting on the assessment.

In summary, both the MMPI and the MBTI are psychological tests that reflect and underscore the value and consequences of the pastor's personality as a nurturer and supporter of others, of being a pleasant, easy-going leader, if not a cheerleader. The typical pastor also has a need to be optimistic about life and interpret problems or conflicts in positive and socially acceptable ways. It is difficult for most pastors, first, to admit to conflict; second, to identify areas where conflict exists; and, finally, to act without a heightened level of stress and anxiety caused by fears that pastoral initiative in conflict resolution may introject hurt, pain, and emotional suffering.

The Strengths and Needs of the Clergy Personality Typologies. In addition to the more clinical descriptions of the benefits and consequences of clergy as high-level nurturers and their need to interpret life positively—thereby minimizing conflicts—other aspects of the pastor's personality are worth noting. Consistent with the high nurturing profile of the pastor is low hostility and a generally low level of suspicion and paranoia. Pastors as a group seem evenly divided in their social anxiety profiles.

Many pastors are of a personality type that allows them to process or deny conflicts with a minimum of social anxiety. They appear relaxed and self-confident. Further, if administrative tasks of ministry are not taken care of, well, they simply aren't taken care of. Other pastors become socially anxious and try too strenuously to resolve their anxiety through frivolous actions. Generally, however, pastors do not have a high level of hostility, suspicion, or social anxiety. Nor as a whole do they tend to be socially aggressive, as suggested in their ranking on the Ma scale of the MMPI. The typical pastor is not a social reformer, not overly aggressive, egotistical, or socially irritable. They tend to be pleasant, outgoing, and adaptable with a realistic perception of reality and social structures. Except under high situational stress factors, they perceive that they are fairly well understood by both families and churches.

A typical conflict between churches and pastors rises when the congregation wants a pastor who is a nurturer of those already within the church and at the same time socially aggressive in evangelism and church growth. To locate the pastor who does both well (scores high on the Mf scale and on the Ma scale) is indeed difficult and would be a rare find. Most churches and pastors fall somewhere between those extremes. Each will have to compromise. If the parties remain conflicted over pastoral expectations, ensuing heightened anxiety of the pastor will probably create problems for the pastor, the congregation, and the pastor's family.

A general concern and conflict between occupation and personal needs occurs over the issue of how one is nurtured personally. One frustrated pastor comments:

> Often I feel I am being used in the sense of being abused because I've determined to serve Christ. What hurts is that the abuse is by those who are in the [denominational] leadership and general membership of Christ's church. Sometimes it seems that those whom I respect as denominatonal leaders don't care about what is happening in my life and are not sympathetic or caring, even about the parishes I serve. We haven't much. It seems each year we have less. People no longer care for the pastor and family as friends or spiritual leaders. You're an employee and they expect you to function as they must in their vocations.

This pastor voices frustrations that rise because not all that he wants for support and nurture is available for him. He wants financial security *and* tender loving care by local as well as denominational church leaders as a single, unified expression of their love for him.

Making Time for the Family. Because the life of many pastors occurs within the neurotic triad where conflicts are resolved in socially acceptable solutions, the complaints, disappointments, and demands of family are felt most acutely. Uniformly across the surveyed denominations, pastors express the need to spend more time with family, and they feel guilty over not managing to obtain high-quality family life. Many clergy reflect sadly on their inability to interpret effectively and meaningfully at home the economic realities of a given congregation. This strained silence heightens the family's frustration and resentment toward the congregation and the denomination. However, a number of pastors comment positively on the support that congregations in the Christian community have afforded them. A United Methodist pastor writes glowingly:

> A very important impact on the family at the time of my first wife's death was the immediate support, community of caring, that surrounded all of us. I believe being in the ministry made that the unique, valuable experience it was even in our deep grieving.

At a time of personal and family crisis, this congregation in its nurture and care was able to respond to the pastor's need in a gratifying and affirming way.

A Presbyterian pastor, in pursuing his own need for nurture, resolved the conflict between church and family by choosing the church:

> The ministry per se, is not so much a factor, as the attitude I took into my role as minister. I believe I turned to the ministry for self-fulfillment rather than to my family. My identity focused on my being a minister first. The role of husband and father became secondary. Reflecting on my past attitudes, I have found that the ministry, while a very rewarding career and vocation, is a singularly unfulfilling one on a personal, family, and social level.

In this pastor's case, turning to the ministry for love, nurture, and self-fulfillment led to separation from his wife, an unsurprising consequence. In effect the pastor became married to the church and not the family. In the recent book *Life in a Glass House* is an insightful discussion of the psychological triangle among the pastor, family, and congregation.[4] Family members feel deeply the impact of the pastor's emotional energies being dedicated solely to the church and their receiving very little attention, care, nurture, and concern. The negative consequences are entirely predictable.

Likewise, a Presbyterian Church of America pastor offers the philosophical observation that his self-esteem and the needs of his family are nurtured and satisfied through his ministry. Their low frustration and deep satisfaction with a low-paying congregation contrasts with many pastors who may think high income eliminates family stress. He says:

> My family knows that I am very human—with all the many pitfalls. Yet they feel that I am one of the best of those at doing the

Lord's work, especially since I could have been much better off financially in another profession.

A fellow PCA pastor reflects the same sense of mutuality between family and the congregation in his comments:

> I love the gospel ministry. I would not want to be anywhere else. The Lord provides our needs constantly, and I love nothing better than to see his kingdom being built. The impact on our family has been positive. Our kids have been a special place in the heart of our congregation, and that has been a real blessing for them.

Whether these two pastors reflect accurately upon a spontaneous mutual nurturing or whether they are mirrors of the dreaded neurotic triad that denies conflict is open to interpretation. The survey responses indicate that these two church/family relationships are mutually satisfying.

A Lutheran pastor captures the positive relationship of pastor, family, and church in his brief comment:

> My family has been very supportive and proud of my ministry.

In summary, clergy obviously do not all share the same psychological profile. Not all personality profiles overlap and great dissimilarity is seen even within the main categories discussed here. Our concern is the general profile of the psychological strengths and needs of pastors. Interactions between pastors with these profiles and their congregations and with their families suggest predictable conflicts and affirmations. A key ingredient to successful nurturing of the pastor's personality occurs when neither the congregation nor the family puts undo pressure on the pastor to perform everything perfectly. When perfectionism is allowed to become dominant, the resultant pressure builds a denial system. On the surface positive results will be evident. But the long-term adverse impact cannot be dismissed. Perfectionism and denial can be ignored only at great peril to ministry. The pastor, family, and church all need nurture, but they must learn to nurture each other without insisting that everything be perfect. Sometimes the optimism and naïve stubbornness of pastors do little to encourage the realistic support and nurture that can be offered them by both family and congregation.

Nurturing Theological Priorities

Receiving Grace From God the Holy Spirit. Pastors who look upon their ministry as a profession and not as a spiritual vocation have embraced a cognitive, rational, objectifying Western theology that emphasizes observable results. They speak in terms of managerial language and skills and minimize the work of the Holy Spirit. Yet receiving grace from the Holy Spirit results in miracle growth for spiritual priorities. How the results are achieved remains ineffable, mysterious, charismatic, mystical, and delightful.

Among pastors who welcome spiritual miracle growth energy from the Holy Spirit, we find an open, intuitive, and vital reciprocity of communication among the pastor, spouse, and family. Here one finds a positive affirmation of the ministry. An American Baptist pastor says of the miracle growth of his calling:

> Great environment for extended, spiritual family and children's and youth programs.

Another American Baptist pastor affirms the same sense of growth, vitality, and ease in ministry:

> My family has enjoyed the church but never been overwhelmed by unreasonable demands. I've made the practice of never doing "church work" at home until the children are in bed. It's been fun!

These pastors reflect in general their sense of high, positive valuing of a call into ministry.

A Lutheran pastor observed:

> Communication between the two of us [husband and wife] is crucial. In that way we know what each other is thinking and feeling and we can make adjustments or explain the problem/tension that is occurring. Both of us are working this year, and our adjustment to that is difficult. Family life is much more interesting with teenagers who share new insights and challenging ideas. I am much more effective as a pastor/pastoral counselor because I have gone through most of the family life cycle with my children.

And a fellow Lutheran minister reports:

> The children are happy about [the ministry] and happy for me because I love my call as a pastor. My husband tries to go along with me, but he is accustomed to my presence [at home]. He and I

are from an era that didn't ordain women, and this particular field of ministry has me in a leadership role he resents. He accepts it intellectually but not emotionally.

Pastors who look upon ministry as an expression of God's grace and report a happy, congenial, mutual reciprocity as well as a deep understanding among the church family and family of marriage do not express either their ministerial affirmations or disappointments in terms of finances, getting ahead, or by negative comparison with other professionals. The unstated assumption for these pastors bears repeating: *God's grace transcends graduate school, qualifying examinations for ordination, an attractive fringe-benefit package, and detailed contractual agreements between the pastor and the church.* Pastors who have received the miracle of spiritual nurture from the Holy Spirit radiate his power to family and to church.

Spiritual and Experiential Theology. Some pastors receive their experiential theology through the Sacraments; others through the charismatic gifts of ministry and glossolalia; still others incorporate an indistinct actualization of the Holy Spirit that transcends the confines of a clearly written job description.

Some of the most satisfying experiences are reported by pastors from the Assemblies of God, a Pentecostal group; and the Nazarenes and the Church of God (Anderson, Indiana), Wesleyan Holiness denominations. The deepest resentment and bitterness toward ministry are exhibited by those who have the best financial incentives. Some of the best-paid pastors among Presbyterians, United Methodists, United Church of Christ people, and Episcopalians appear least receptive to spiritual and experiential dimensions of life. Implications from our studies of the eleven denominations are clear. Pastors open to receiving the spiritual nurture of God's Holy Spirit establish their theological priorities first. They integrate best the experiential, spiritual, and family communications; and enjoy positive relations with congregations. These pastors report the least amount of stress in their institutional responsibilities and their family relationships. Their personal self-identity as human beings and pastors is essentially positive.

A further implication is seen among pastors whose theological tradition is more open to a specific spiritual calling. These pastors express an almost mystical sense of pastoring that transcends job descriptions or contractually binding financial agreements. We are not suggesting that job descriptions and contractual agreements should not exist. However, the foundation upon which effective ministry begins is a spiritual, charismatic, mystical relationship with God that transcends efforts to codify ministry in managerial language.

The pastor who is unable to transcend contractual-agreement language has rationalized and reduced pastoral ministry-specific operational functions. We can predict conflicts and struggles with self, church, and family for that pastor. The theological perspective offered by the biblical sense of vocation affirms that God calls through the Holy Spirit, not through labor negotiations. Unless spiritual and experiential dimensions are incorporated, one can predict that the pastor will have difficulties with self, the immediate family, the extended family of the congregation, and ultimately the denomination.

We cited earlier the UCC pastor who explains this dilemma well:

> I have promised myself that I will never have children because I don't want to subject children to the kind of [religious] environment I grew up in. I'm the kind of minister who would put the church first over family, so I've decided not to have a family. Also, my prospects for marriage are very slim because I am a minister. Most men cannot deal with that. I am reconciled to that fact and usually comfortable with my circumstances.

Here is a pastor who is frustrated and negative on both major aspects of her life. One easily detects bitterness and resentment toward the experiential dimensions of being a minister. Second, she projects her negative feelings in her statement that no reasonable, emotionally mature man would want to marry a minister. Her bitterness both with the family of God and the family of marriage are overwhelming to her. Experientially, little is integrated in her life, and one senses that she has not experienced much miracle growth.

Nurture Intention. One goal of maturity in ministry is to increase the capacity of the nurturing pastor to tolerate frustration and tension. Conflict, tension, and a hostile or uncaring work environment are the sources of greatest stress and tension. One Church of God pastor summarizes the dilemma well:

Probably my problems with stress are self-imposed. I expect too much of myself. Others' expectations may not be so extreme as my own. At times this will impact my family in various ways.

Another Church of God pastor shared this sense of dealing with the tensions of ministry in a constructive way:

I have tried to make our family like a normal Christian home, and our children act like any children their age. Our standards at home are no higher than the biblical expectations for all Christians. The greatest stress comes from pressure on my wife to be supportive and sense problems between the people and me.

These pastors are not naïve about tensions that exist, but they are integrating the nurturing support of spiritual and experiential dimensions and are able to express in constructive and realistic ways the benefits and tensions of being in ministry.

A Nazarene pastor puts the spiritual capstone on the miracle-growth aspect of ministry in his reflections:

If God had not called me—if I were not a hundred percent sure he had—I'd be a carpenter again. But even with the problems, the greatest place in all the world is to be in the center of God's will.

The secret of success in ministry is the psychological and experiential capacity to integrate the spiritual dimensions of God's call. Pastors who report most positively on their ministry reveal an experiential capacity for open communications with their spouses and do not project unrealistic and destructive expectations upon their children. Further, they do not ascribe the sources of life's tensions and frustrations to the congregation. Where the integration of spiritual and experiential dimensions occurs, one feels the support and nurture that all pastors yearn to receive from the congregation, the family (both spouse and children), and from one's inner sense of well-being and satisfaction that one is called to be a minister and not something else.

The Continuing Need to Prune Old Priorities

Job Limits. No spiritual, family, or occupational relationship exists without the necessity of new boundaries. Pastors have continually to prune new growth in order to ensure long-term, orderly ministry. Pastors who experience a rich infusion of spiritual miracle growth may believe their ministry will be perpetually blessed. For example, a pastor may have done well in small churches and then moves to a larger one. He/she must be careful not to project previous growth and development onto a linear-scale model that shows automatic church growth, guaranteed affirmation, ever-increasing benefits, and assurance of joyful spiritual leadership. Alas! The pruning begins.

Perhaps the "cutting away" comes from a family health problem or a stubborn and recalcitrant church or failure to achieve the success that one had enjoyed in a different sociological situation or an extremely difficult and complex set of expectations and lack of affirmation in a larger church. The need to see that children and spouse complete their education may delay the plans for further education for the pastor or push career advancement further into the future. These responsibilities are all forms of pruning.

The pruning process, despite its initial outward ugly appearance, is not an absolute loss of vitality, growth, significance, and satisfaction. Rather, pruning is God's way or the congregation's means or the family need to declare limits to one's ministry and career motivation. Those limits may manifest themselves in a variety of ways. For example, a Disciples pastor says:

> During part of my ministry, we lived among people who had a higher income than we did. Though our children had never been deprived by any objective standards, they felt deprived on a comparative basis.

Fortunately this pastor has the professional and spiritual maturity to understand that his children's negative comparison was between himself and a relatively affluent congregational context. The pastor and his family could see that the pruning has brought maturity to him, his family, and especially his children.

Another Disciples pastor reflects on a more negative reaction to the continuing pruning process:

> I've been divorced over four years. The counseling I sought after divorce enabled me to become much less manipulative a person, with a high degree of self-respect and more realistic view of members. They do not disappoint me anymore. Who knows whether I would have grown into the healthy person I am today without the crisis that divorce precipitated in my life/ministry?

This is at once a painful assessment and an affirmation of the pruning process. The same pastor goes on to say:

> I'm happy, effective, and deeply grateful that I've finally become pretty good at what I do.

Indeed, a painful pruning occurred, but for this pastor the process was one that brought with it post-divorce positive benefits for all, including, he claims in other comments, his former wife.

Learning To Say No. No growth is unrestrained. Cultivation, pruning, limit setting, and learning to accept the vicissitudes of life are all are part of both personal, spiritual, and family maturity. As nurturers, clergy do not like to say no to anything, especially wherever pain occurs or the nurturing pastor believes there is a way to solve the problem in question. The measure of one's spiritual and professional maturity is the ability to say no occasionally, even to situations where the pastor might be able to help; and of learning not to look for a silver lining in every cloud. Learning to say no is a measure of maturity not defeat.

A single UCC clergywoman expresses the dilemma of needing to say no:

> The major impact is that I often put my congregation's or denomination's needs over my personal needs and those of family. In terms of developing my own family, being a parish minister isn't exactly conducive to meeting people or dating. My prime working time is others' leisure time [weekends and evenings].

There is, of course, a simple solution to this pastor's dilemma. She identifies her struggle but overlooks her inability to say no to congregational expectations, which she would like to do so that she could enjoy positive social and dating relationships. In all likelihood, the flock takes advantage of her singleness. Not yet bitter but frustrated, this pastor needs to receive and apply the pruning treatment both to herself and her congregation.

Setbacks Can Be Steps Forward. The image of pruning is just that, *pruning.* Nurturers do not like to hurt or to be hurt. Whenever pruning occurs, there is hurt and setback. However, the first blush of a painful, disappointing setback may well be the pruning necessary for positive growth. One United Methodist pastor reflects on this dilemma philosophically:

I sacrificed my family in their growing years for the work of the church. I felt guilty choosing the family over the church. Consequently, I missed seeing my children in some school activities and sporting events. I learned too late that the church can and does survive well without the pastor. In the early years of ministry, struggling for success, security, building confidence in one's ability, I think the pastor tends to sacrifice the family.

Pruning is never pleasant, but it is necessary for personal growth and family growth and maturity as well as for the spiritual development of a pastor in any church situation.

Keeping Ministry in Perspective

Changing Social Perceptions of the Minister's Family. In the twenty-five years since William Douglas' classic study, *Ministers' Wives*, many changes have occurred. For example, in 1965 Douglas assumed that the pastor's spouse was female. The bulk of respondents in his study indicated that the wife was seen as a partner in ministry or as one who lovingly provides support. Few spouses/wives were "detached in principle."[5] Our study shows remnants of that perspective still existent in some churches.

A Nazarene pastor reports:

The ministry has strengthened our marriage, and the constant struggles unite us. I could not minister without [my wife]. She is God's primary human resource to renew, refresh, and encourage me.

Correspondingly, a Presbyterian minister expresses the homogeneity of thought and organic unity of family, work, and spirituality in his observation:

I think overall that my being a minister has had a positive effect on our family. Our kids are committed to Christ. The ministry has provided many very special opportunities for me to be involved with them because of a flexible work schedule, more than in any other occupation. I enjoy my family and we've tried overall to put God first, family second, and employment at the church third. I feel we've been successful at this.

Here the male is leader and declares that God is first, family second, and congregation third. And everyone is happy. In family-systems theory, this is known as "triangulation." While this Presbyterian's report may be accurate and the diagnosis of his success in ministry correct, we doubt that this organic unity is an accurate representation for many pastors in the denominations studied. Few pastors or their families share this Presbyterian pastor's list of priorities. Likewise, many congregations do not share in that pastor's set of theological priorities.

For Douglas the prevailing model for the pastor's perception of work and family relations is what might be called the "organic unity" model. This model assumes a unity of work, economy, call/ministry, and institutional ministry. Most likely the rural setting was a predominant social setting model, whether or not ministry was actually performed in a rural setting. The so-called Protestant work ethic, the organic unity of work, person, family, and beliefs in the mid-sixties, despite all the revolutionary political reactions of that period, was a fairly prevalent and cohesive model.

In the Douglas model, the pastor is male and works out of a hierarchical model within an overall context of organic unity of basic functions. In that context, the wife submits willingly and obediently to the pastor/husband and the church at large. Religion was perceived as integral to and interwoven with any organic unity of work, family dedication, salary, and benefits. By 1990, one finds in *Life in a Glass House* that language about the minister's family shifts from the wife perceiving her role in hierarchical subordination or organic-unity model of ministry to a more sociological perspective. The authors observe a three-way conflict of pastor, family, and church—triangulation. In the Douglas model, therapeutic attention extends beyond conflict between husband and wife to include church work and life. In triangular conflict the church is regarded as a corporate personality, the minister is the second party, and the family (or spouse) is the third partner.

A second major triangulation shift relates to spiritual-life realities of culture and pastors. The spiritual homogeneity or spiritual organic unity of a congregation, a pastor, and a pastor's family can no longer be assumed. A congregation may have a divided, albeit creative, mixture of charismatics and non-charismatics; likewise, the pastor may hold theological loyalties and commitments that vary considerably from the congregation's. And the pastor's spouse or family members may hold theological views that differ from both the pastor's and the congregation's.

The advent of liturgical renewal brought a substantial shift in spiritual expression that was not included in or anticipated by the Douglas book's perspective on spirituality.

The shift toward an egalitarian marriage model in the 1990s is, in our judgment, a positive change. In divorced clergy families, single parenting, stepchildren and stepparents, and child-care responsibilities radically alter, for most pastors, the hierarchical or organic unity model common twenty-five years ago. The pastor's family of the 1990s may be fragmented in its beliefs, work responsibilities, and acceptance of traditional family functions such as child care, cooking, and income production. The egalitarian model, in which husband and wife have equal or shared roles, differs sharply from the organic unity model where the minister's wife shares in his work and uncritically bonds with the church.

Religion no longer is seen as a unifying experience for the clergy family as it was in 1965. William Everett, in his study, "The Faith of Couple Careers: Exploring Alternative Vocational Patterns,"[6] suggests that for an increasingly large percentage of the population, particularly where dual-career or dual-worker marriages are involved, religion is considered a leisure-time activity. The pastor, especially one in a dual-career marriage, cannot count on religion as the cohesive force in marriage. In fact, religion may fragment both life and marriage. Religion as leisure-time activity in egalitarian marriages suggests a decreased amount of family time spent in devotions, Bible study at home, or family participation in church activities. Church school educators corroborate this trend. They report that both children and adults are less knowledgeable about the Bible, use religious language less often when discussing moral issues, and tend to distance themselves from religious activities; they regard "church" as simply another option.

These changes create a two-source stresser for the clergy family: the pastor's spouse as a partner in ministry is not valued as a spiritual model by church members, and the role of religion in the minister's family may become more fragmented, less organic, and more specialized. Spiritual certainty that seemed so well established in 1965 is not at all secure in the 1990s. Further, ministry is perceived very differently by clergy responding to our survey from clergy participating in the William Douglas sample.

Evidence points toward a double triangular conflict among ministers' families: (a) church–family–pastor and (b) religion as leisure–family as committed to egalitarian norms–pastor as spiritual nurturer in conflict with spouse as egalitarian mate. As more women expect an egalitarian model in their marriages and employment, whether as pastors or pastors' spouses, the old organic-unity, hierarchical model of ministry and marriage will generate more and more theological and sociological stress. Theological stress is far more evident in the 1990s than in 1965, and the sociological conflict of triangulation is obvious. The theological conflict also forces a spiritual triangulation.

Under the organic-unity model of ministry, we have the comments of a Church of God pastor who is typical of this perspective:

> Pastoring has been very positive for my family. The church is our extended family and has been extremely supportive.

However, a fellow Church of God pastor reveals some of the theological as well as sociological tension in his movement away from the organic model:

> It was hard to answer the question on the family because our children are grown and on their own. My wife and I have a very good, open relationship at this time. The only thing that disturbs me is that she has to work outside the home.

In the first of the two quotes, the minister reveals an organic unity of social, economic, work, and marital integrity. The second minister reveals more conflict. Indeed, his children are gone and one would think at that point the financial stress would be less. However, either in efforts to recoup financial losses or to begin to enjoy the marriage partnership or perhaps because the clergy's spouse wants to work outside the home, the pastor expresses sociological and theological conflict over his wife having to "work outside the home."

Maintaining the Big Picture Without Forgetting Details. Pastors tend to be organic-unity professionals. Most pastors do not think of personal life and family as being in opposition to the work of ministry. Both the family and the ministry nurture the pastor. Traditionally, pastors' families have willingly accepted the role of primary nurturer of the pastor. However, as the culture moves away from an organic-unity perception of work and family toward a more egalitarian or even fragmented understanding of work and family ties, a family and a theological cleavage result. No longer does a comfortable unity of family and congregation exist for the pastor. Everett suggests that the predominance of baby boomers in churches is making religion primarily a leisure option. But for the pastor and the dedicated church-goer, religion is not an option; it is essential. For some pastors, conflict rises from the tension between a close bond of pastor and church and the opposition they experience from spouse and family.

In summary, twenty-five years ago the organic-unity model of ministry encouraged pastors to assume that family and occupation were the same thing. In the 1990s the complexity of ministry, changes in the workplace, marriage, and dual-career couples require the clergy, the clergy family, and indeed the congregation to be more sociologically and theologically astute in differentiating between family and church priorities in ministry.

The Temptation To Overfocus. Conflict exists in clergy families where the pastor refuses or otherwise fails to see that the clergy family is no longer unified in respect to the call to ministry and dedication to the congregation. When such conflict exists and the pastor nonetheless reports close ties to the congregation, we hypothesize that the closeness is not one of theological unanimity or even harmony. The pastor simply receives emotional support from highly positive, visible activities within the congregation to take the place of support that the family fails to give. But the pastor must come to understand that the relationship to the congregation cannot substitute for love and encouragement from the family. Conflict between pastor and family will only increase.

Lost in the Woods. Where church activities are seen as the primary support for the pastor, one can surmise that the pastor has lost his or her way maritally. Church activities themselves are the affirmation for the pastor. Lacking is a theological perspective on implications of a divine call to ministry, a perspective in which congregational activities and the pastor's ministerial strengths and his family are seen as complementary ties.

In a less egalitarian culture, the spouse and family might be more willing to acquiesce to the pastor's being lost in the professional woods of church-related activities. After all, the family may rationalize, the minister's call is the priority and who among the family dare challenge that theological truth? This is the typical traditional rationale. But nowadays pastors' spouses and family members are becoming more theologically sophisticated and self-critical and have developed the capacity to separate personal issues from spiritual priorities. These families show less patience with, less professional indulgence of, and greater stress from financial and theological conflicts. If the pastor fails to develop a mature perspective and subordinate church activities and place more value on family relationships, the family is likely to become bothersome and secondary. When this dynamic is allowed to flourish, both ministry and family are endangered.

Family Activities as Support. For many pastors, spending time with the family does not assume the same value as "working." Participation in family activities requires emotional involvement, not just time and ideas. The problem is expressed by the pastor who asks, "What would we do if I had a day off?" Often this comment is followed by disparaging asides about inadequate time, finances, clothes, and transportation—or a long litany of negatives that preclude quality time with the family. These negative reactions against spending time with the family reveal a pastor's conflict over drawing appropriate support from and giving valuable support to the family in a non-work and unstructured situation.

Family members want their own autonomy, not in defiance of the pastor but because they need to put the emotional and spiritual trees and the forest in perspective. If the pastor spends too much time with the family, then the pastor ignores the forest that is the church. Many pastors in our survey have in retrospect reflected upon the loss of or failure to develop good family relations. Once the problem is discovered and identified, they fear it is too late, or they doubt their ability to be intimate with their families. One Presbyterian minister shares his own conflict:

> The impact of being a minister in a small community means that I have no social life and therefore little opportunity of ever having a family.

This single pastor despairs of the possibility of her achieving a healthful perspective in which family priorities can survive or flourish in ministry.

An Episcopal priest takes a more activist and affirming role when he observes:

> The flexibility of my schedule gives me time with my kids that many other fathers don't enjoy. I can also plan vacation time around the needs of our extended families. Of course, there is a price to pay in my being gone a lot in the evenings.

We see a healthful, integrated perspective in this clergyman. He understands well that one cannot live without conflict and that there "is a price to pay" for time spent with the family. The healthful perspective of not overfocusing either on family opportunities lost or the devastating inextricable demands of the congregation is a measure of theological maturity and an appropriate theological assessment and differentiation of role function.

A Diversity Model. A means of not overfocusing on church support or family support is to affirm that the task of the moment is in fact the calling. This model retains a self-critical perspective that allows one to give one hundred percent to either church or family activity. A selective cutting back and regrouping is in order. The image for ministry in the 1990s suggests that alongside a mature ministry and congenial family relations are undeveloped possibilities for new forms of ministry and family life. The mature pastor is able to keep life, work, and love in perspective. No longer is visible unity required between the minister/congregation and minister/family because the pastor cannot simultaneously devote a hundred percent to both church and family.

We are suggesting that the pastor must have a mixture of church and family, church and pastor, pastor and spouse, and pastor and children. The relationship of these various entities or aspects of the pastor's life provides a new diversity. Ministry in the 1990s is not so uniform as the old organic-unity model nor so selective that it alienates and fragments family and work functions. The diversity model allows the pastor freely to enjoy family, spouse, and children as well as the congregation and individual members without destroying or threatening other relationships. The pastor in this model is not one who controls either church or family. Nor does the church or the family control the pastor.

Church as Community in Perspective. An immediate implication of this model suggests that the basic social and spiritual needs of laity and clergy are met within the organized structural unity of the church. Personification of the church as leader and community minimizes the autonomy of the minister, family, and indeed individual church members. There may be a basic cohesiveness in the church as community, but it is not and cannot be all-encompassing. The temptation to take flight into the liturgical life of the church as community is dangerous because the church would then become a surrogate or substitute for healthful attachments to other activities, tasks, accomplishments, and individuals outside the church.

Egalitarian marriages are on the rise; therefore, one must also surmise that egalitarian church-membership relations are on the rise. That means fewer people will be at the church whenever the doors open. By the same token, we will expect to find fewer people maintaining church membership but more actually participating. As the culture comes to understand religion as a leisure activity, both congregation and pastor will have more freedom and power to enable church members to make more discerning and cohesive commitments to church life.

The pastor who is unable to see his or her relationship to the church as a type of spiritual egalitarian marriage is in trouble. The pastor who is in a marriage where egalitarian dimensions are disruptive or fragmenting rather than renewing, invigorating, and inviting will have difficulty achieving open communication with family members. For these pastors, understanding the church as community will be even more complicated, and that perspective will become a probable source of both theological and sociological frustration.

Learning to minister in the church as community calls for the pastor to foster increased commitment. In addition, the pastor will have to develop an increased tolerance of conflict and ambivalence among the church members as well as with his or her family members. The laity in secular settings are learning to make radical differentiations in their lives and commitments. Where marriage partners develop an increased emphasis upon intimate communication, they report better marriages and better work relationships. When this dynamic is applied to the church's need to build community through intimate communication, one finds small-group prayer meetings and Bible studies. The result is greater involvement in the total life of the church. Increasing one's capacity to make commitments that involve intimate communication is necessary if fragmentation of church and family is to be overcome.

As a pastor learns to relate to the church as community by helping it to distinguish between global and specific commitments, the pastor will, we believe, build a more cohesive community both within the church and the minister's own marriage. More open communication between pastor and church, pastor and family, and family and church will avoid a situation where pastor and church face off against the family or pastor and family cross swords with the church. A Presbyterian minister summarizes this dilemma and its outcome in a succinct way:

> In my other profession, no one noticed that [my wife] was not a "coworker."

This minister points out for many pastors the dilemma and the possibility of resolving it.

One can be an effective pastor without forcing the spouse to be an unrecognized coworker. At the same time, the pastor must become less defensive, less evasively involved with the family, and take more personal and theological responsibility for addressing the tasks and activities of ministry. The pastor must do this without compelling the family to act as a buffer between oneself and the church or evading responsibility for effective ministry by cowering behind a shield of family concerns.

4

From Call to Pulpit

In this chapter we examine the issues a pastor and family must evaluate, beginning with the time a prospective pastor first clearly discerns a call into pastoral ministry. Then we will look at the effects upon and the processes through which the family moves in response to the call. Further, we examine practical considerations and sacrifices involved in progressing from call to pulpit. Finally, we want to suggest ways spiritual mentors, supervisors, or "elders of the faith" offer spiritual guidance to the fledgling pastor. As an addendum, we will mention "incidentals" in the move from call to pulpit that often become more significant than they might at first appear to be.

How the Call Comes

Spiritual Considerations. A pastor's discernment of God's call may come suddenly or dawn gradually. The process by which one moves away from earlier life plans, commitments, careers, and educational pursuits toward ministry involves a long, often tortuous but needful spiritual pilgrimage to sort the wheat from the chaff of one's initial awareness of the call into full-time pastoral ministry. Most pastors do not follow the Pauline example of a three-year sojourn in the desert or of Jesus' forty days and nights in the wilderness. But each pastor who exhibits any spiritual maturity will begin a thorough, thoughtful, and prayerful consideration of what being called into ministry means. The initial stage is opening the door of one's life to the

71

call. This stage is unequivacally spiritual: "Yes! God has called me and wants me for this unique form of service."

Under the head of spiritual considerations, some mention of the analogy to mystical experience may also be appropriate. A period of self-examination and even of self-doubt or self-dismissal follows, as seen in Moses' efforts to disqualify himself from leadership of the children of Israel from Egypt because of a speech impediment. But God persisted: "[Aaron] shall speak for you to the people; and he shall be a mouth for you, and you shall be to him as God" (Ex. 4:16). It is as though God said, "When I call, I provide all you will need."

As one consolidates within one's mind and spirit the dramatic implications of a call to minstry, the called must then turn to family considerations. How does this call affect spouse, parents, children, or marital plans?

Family Considerations. Our survey indicates that a large percentage of spouses knew that he or she was marrying a minister. Only 237 (thirty-four percent) did not know the spouse planned to go into the ministry, while 459 (sixty-five percent) did know. This suggests that many pastors receive their call fairly early in life. Or they have a deep and sufficiently active religious commitment so that the spouse is not surprised by the decision, whether it comes toward the end of high school, college, graduate school, or early in one's secular career. When pastors who were either divorced or separated were asked whether the marriage failure resulted from being in ministry, fifty-seven (seventy percent) of eighty-one reported that it did not. Here are two significant facts: A high percentage of spouses knew that their marriage partner was entering the ministry; of those that ended in divorce or separation, less than a third identify ministry as a factor in the divorce. These findings suggest a high degree of continuity between the pastor's own processing of a call and the family's understanding of or willingness to support the marriage partner or family member in ministry.

Pastors' comments indicate that the more clearly the call is discerned by the pastor and the more thoroughly the decision is processed by the family, the higher the level of support for ministry and the less likely the family is to be harshly surprised by the realities of ministry. Practical considerations such as church-owned or private housing, the "household environment" of neighborhood, school district, cost of living, proximity to medical facilities and cultural activities are all important for the family. If the pastor is sensitive to their concerns, the more supportive the family is of the pastor's role as shepherd of God's flock.

The immediate contextual factor of the pastor's household environment extends into issues of career-path trajectories, financial limitations of the ministry, and the fact that one is called to sacrifice in ministry. Approximately forty-four percent of spouses reported that they find it necessary to work to make ends meet. By and large, families know that this sacrifice is by definition what ministry is and are willing to make appropriate personal sacrifices, including the need for spouses to work. By contrast, an effort to try ministry because it is something different and has humanitarian value through assisting people in their various needs is a decision based on spurious vocational considerations. Missing is an understanding of the sacrificial nature of ministry. Correspondingly, where the transition is not spiritually clear for the pastor, the family also receives mixed messages and conflicted promises and is far less certain, capable, and willing to follow the pastor down another turn in the road of life.

A justified inference can be drawn from our findings. The more carefully and thoroughly the pastor understands that ministry is a spiritual call primarily between the pastor and God, the most secure the marriage. We have shown that when theological and familial issues have been openly discussed among family members, the pastor and the family will experience less stress than those who ignore or take lightly either spiritual or family commitments.

Vocational Considerations. If the call to ministry comes early in life, vocational realities of starting at the bottom and progressing ever so slowly are probably easier to accept and to aspire to. Those who enter the ministry having already been actively involved in a non-ministerial career, will probably find the change in vocations more complex and troublesome. Two warnings must be noted by those who have heard the call and contemplate a change from an established, successful career, especially if from a service-related job. If one is established in a career trajectory that is in other than a not-for-profit organization, financial disparities between secular and pastoral work may be substantial. The second warning is whether the would-be pastor is actually responding to God's call or suffering from career burnout, fatigue, boredom, or an employment shift in the industry. If a pastor's contemplated change is not based on spiritual considerations but on vocational adjustment conflicts, everyone beware!

Our surveys and interviews suggest that the easiest transition is made by those who receive a call and decide to enter the ministry at successful mid-career points in other vocational paths. Basically they understand the sacrifices entailed (economic, family dislocation, setting aside of a certain lifestyle, and minimal professional perks). The family senses the clear-cut positive vocational decision and tends to be supportive, although perhaps mystified by such a radical career change. The more difficult transition occurs among those who are simply burned out, bored, or angry at their failure to advance as rapidly as they had thought in the former career path. The minister, by stark contrast with those in the electronic, medical, and high-tech career fields, exists in what sociologists call an age-graded or traditional culture. This means that regardless of how bright or able one is, an extended apprenticeship of five to twenty years occurs before one may reasonably expect to be in a position to pastor a "high-steeple church" or to be in a position of significant public leadership within the denomination.

Finally, the interweaving of spiritual, family, and vocational considerations must be done holistically. The call comes from spiritual realities, through family members, and through specific vocational opportunities. Neglecting any one of these three matrices or emphasizing only one to the exclusion of the other two signals a rocky road from call to pulpit.

Formulating Commitments

Commitment to Education in Training. In the move from one's personal call into ministry to the point of taking pastoral responsibility in a pulpit involves some form of formal education. It may be a seminary degree, a diploma from a Bible college, or a certificate from correspondence courses. Certainly it will involve the educational preparation necessary to pass an ordination committee whether that committee is comprised of laity of a local church or bishops or pastors. The educational preparation is not limited strictly to formal classroom work, but it includes indoctrination in the history, polity, and theology of the individual faith group. And it will certainly involve the preparation needed to pass peer review. Pastoring is a sacred privilege in each denomination, and the church guards that right in its own distinctive theological way.

A perpetual conflict exists between a formal education that may rob the future pastor of spiritual life and enthusiasm and, on the other hand, a disregard for education and the wisdom of spiritual elders that preserves a robust and charismatic zeal for ministry. Trouble for the move from call to pulpit resulting from ignorance is not to be preferred over trouble rising from education in an academic world that may be antagonistic to one's personal faith. Parishioners expect their pastor to be knowledgeable about the history, polity, and doctrines of their denomination and to live faithfully and consistently in and out of the pulpit in keeping with those doctrinal standards and expectations. Several hypotheses suggest themselves: 1) Some component of formal education, academic classroom work, is essential; 2) meditative, soul-searching confrontion with one's inner spiritual world is essential; 3) effectively presenting one's self and call to the review of spiritual peers is essential; 4) introduction to the idiosyncrasies of the everyday workplace of parish ministry is essential. The more thorough and thoughtful the pastor's training and preparation are the greater the likelihood of pastoral success. Here success is measured by the capacity to labor effectively in the ministry for thirty or forty years.

The wisdom of a commitment to education is seen in our findings that show nearly forty percent of pastors surveyed changed denominations from faith group of origin to the denomination whose pulpit the pastor occupies currently. This was a higher percentage than we anticipated. The data from the eleven denominations suggest a random movement from one denomination to another. Assemblies of God ministers moved to the United Methodist Church, and Church of God pastors became Episcopal priests. In each of the faith groups one finds this phenomenon. One can only surmise that a number of competing and unpredictable factors of theology, geography, and family commitments are at work here. Unique opportunities in a particular area or denomination seem to inspire folks to leave one denomination to go to another.

Dislocation of Expectations. Whether one makes a commitment to ministry in one's youth or at mid-career, dislocation of expectations occurs for the individual as well as family. The work may be harder than anticipated. The sacrifices may be greater than thought. The rewards may be more elusive than expected. The church may be more of an all-consuming and divisive influence on the pastor's spouse than contemplated.

But in our survey sixty percent of pastors and fifty-five percent of their spouses found the degree of pressure in their first church about as expected. This would suggest that whatever the pastor perceives to be pressure from the ministry is reflected in family comments and expectations. Fifty-five percent added that pressures were not great enough to cause family problems. However, forty-four percent experienced a variety of problems such as financial binds, physical ailments, marital stress, and rebellious children. Forty-seven percent of the pastors reported that their spouses felt pressured to participate in church activities. We anticipated that the figure would be greater.

These findings suggest that as pastors prepare themselves through training, spiritual reflection, conscientious meeting with peer groups and spiritual mentors, and as the families are brought on board regarding the call, relocations are dealt with in a relatively reasonable way. The data suggest that the more open one's spiritual eyes are in the movement from call to pulpit the higher the capacity of the pastor and family to absorb whatever dislocation of expectations they might experience. Correspondingly, as the pastor is able to understand and make definite commitments to the movement from call to pulpit and to explain the transitions that will be necessary, the spouse's needs will be more effectively met.

Unexpected Hurdles. The deepest of callings and the most thorough of training experiences cannot forestall unexpected obstacles. For example an Assemblies of God pastor reports on one of the pressures in his pastorate:

. . . having to relate to people who are not true Christians or who do not live it and who are strong in the church but not in spiritual things.

An Episcopal priest writes of a different hurdle:

In my first assignment I had great difficulty with the rector. He is no longer a pastor.

At a critical juncture in this young priest's ministerial life, he came under the tutelage of a rector who apparently was theologically abusive and cast doubt on the authenticity of the priest's call. However, the young pastor is still a priest, and his first supervising pastor has since left the ministry. In each of these cases, a pastor ran into a different theological and spiritual climate than expected.

A Methodist pastor reports:

At one point my appointment was 165 miles from my spouse's place of work. For two years we commuted to see one another. There was no effective communication and this was leading to divorce.

Four points of concern for this pastor are geography, mileage, fatigue, and alienation. Not many pastors would expect a several-hour commute to the spouse. Visits are infrequent and under a highly stressful time frame. Typically the pastor would have to be in the pulpit on Sunday, which is the time that the spouse has off. Their schedules are difficult to coordinate for good communication, relaxation, and family life.

In summary, one does not make an impulsive leap into ministry believing that if one is called all details are taken care of automatically by the Holy Spirit, benevolent older pastors, sympathetic families, and unlimited amounts of energy.

Practical Considerations

Called to Service. As stated, sociologically the church is an age-graded or tradition-oriented culture. The institution itself changes slowly. The rise to leadership occurs gradually, and the rewards are more intrinsic to the overall life of the community and not to the individual pastor. In short, ministry is not a quick route to fame and fortune. Not only is the church as an institution set up to mitigate those typically individualistic expectations that reside in American culture, but the nature of spiritual call itself is to ministry and humble service.

Further complicating the picture is the fact that educational requirements for ministry are extensive. Therefore, a pastor puts a considerable amount of energy into both formal training and apprenticeship before one has a sense that the pastor's theology and style of ministry are directly affecting the lives of fellow Christians. Whether in professional sports, entertainment, or ministry, a small percentage (one to two percent) achieve those positions and public acclaim that are associated with a given profession. One of the practical considerations in one's call to service is the spiritual principle of "self-limitation." One is called as a minister of the Gospel to act and offer grace in the name of Jesus Christ, God's grace itself. The principle of spiritual self-limitation is a means by which we understand ourselves, the church, and our families, contexts in which we work and serve well and those where we do not do so well.

The parable of the talents in the New Testament is as much about the one-talent as it is about the two- or five-talent servant. Many more one-talent servants and pastors are abroad in the land than are five-talent ones. The call is to use that talent wisely and not to bury it or surrender to disillusionment and bitterness. The different work settings of 1) multiple staff, 2) multiple churches or circuit, and 3) single-church pastorates are viable arenas of ministry. But each has different practical considerations. It may not be spiritually wise or discerning to believe that one's ministry is more effectively carried out in the large multiple-staff church.

One Methodist pastor in living out the principle of self-limitation reported:

> Last year I requested a move from a 550-member successful church to a 300-member church. I was exhausted. Despite the salary cut and some fears that came with it, the change has worked well.

Here is a pastor who has made an unusual move by requesting a move to a smaller church, the "downward mobility of the Gospel." He has in mind the good of the church, his own mental and spiritual health, and, by implication, improved relations with his family. The pastor had the courage to do what many pastors would like to do but fear because of peer pressure, pointing fingers, or a sense of personal failure prevents this type of change. But this pastor evidenced a real sense of call by openly and publicly declaring that his call was to a three hundred- not five hundred-member parish.

Actual Cost/Benefits of Call. The cost of formal training, especially at the seminary level, is significant. In an address to a large gathering of alumni of Duke University Divinity School, Dean Dennis Campbell placed the cost of seminary education in a comparative context:

> Recently I was talking to an alumnus of The Divinity School of twenty-five years ago. The pastor informed me that the year he was graduated the tuition for the entire year was $310, and his first appointment paid $3,100. His starting salary was ten times the tuition of his senior year in seminary. However in 1990 tuition at Duke is over $6,000; and there is no way a pastor is going to receive a starting salary of some $60,000.

Dean Campbell then cited an illustration from President Derek Bok of Harvard University, who declared in a recent speech that when he became president in 1971 a difference in income between a beginning professor at Harvard Law School and a Harvard Law School graduate at a New York law firm was approximately $3,000 to $5,000. In 1990 the difference in salaries was $100,000.

These examples are cited to indicate how expensive seminary education is even by comparison with other professional schools. Resulting benefits are not likely to be seen in a sharply increased capacity to earn income. Rather, a seminary education exists because it is preparation for *ministry*, not because it will guarantee higher wages.

A second cost relates to family disruptions and the high expectations placed upon a pastor's children, both by the family and certainly the local church. One pastor surveyed reported:

> The children resent having to attend services.

Another pastor cited a similar theme:

> Pressures in the ministry led to a near breakdown before I learned to adjust; the family often feels neglected.

A Lutheran pastor reports:

The expectations of me as wife/mother never really changed. My challenge has been to change my role, not be super mom/pastor.

An Assemblies of God pastor comments on the stress on family:

My parents have not always understood why I haven't made more money at times when finances have been tight, but for the most part they are supportive.

An American Baptist pastor relates the same dilemma:

There is not excessive stress, but my daughters sometimes want to make commitments to school activities over church.

These various statements suggest that the lives of the pastor and his/her family as well as pastor's children are so interwoven that neither the spouse nor the children are really able to live lives independent of the pastor's call. There will always be human costs to the family, required sacrifices to support ministry. There are the corresponding financial sacrifices simply because church salaries and benefits are not financially attractive.

A third dilemma has to do with career issues in a dual-career marriage. If one spouse is offered a substantial promotion, what does the family do? Do the spouses take turns, with one sacrificing for the promotion of the other, and then the next time they play turnabout? Or is one spouse's career invariably the favored one? Always sacrifices will have to be made in a dual-career marriage, and probably no more in a pastor's marriage than in other careers. In a dual-career marriage, neither spouse can expect to realize the optimal career promotions that might come.[1]

Much has been written in recent years about the fast track, the "mommy track," the "daddy track," and the need to slow down. The bigger, faster-paced, higher-paying church may not be everyone's spiritual cup of tea. There may be benefits from living in a smaller town, enjoying a slower pace, having more time with the family, and experiencing less stress. But benefit of having more time with family in a slower-paced work situation has its costs because that choice will remove the pastor from the ever-onward-and-upward mobility treadmill. On the other hand, it affirms that ministry occurs *here and now* and not at some illusory point in the future.

The Sacrifice Factor. The professional grass may always be greener on the other side of the fence. The minister will never be an equal with peer professionals in terms of status, income, perks, the capacity to control one's life, gain privacy, protect oneself from a twenty-four-hours-a-day, seven-days-a-week schedule. The pastor in some ways is always on call but is never really paid for it. Peer professionals will always do better from a financial point of view. A pastor's expected income and status can be favorably compared to a public school teacher with comparable years of service.

Our findings suggest further that, though during the first five years of ministry financial benefits may be comparable to peer professionals, an ever-increasing "payback" disparity exists between the ministry and other peer professions. For example, while attorneys, physicians, and business school grads also have to amortize their significant graduate school expenses and start-up business costs, eventually their client base will decrease their fixed costs. Perhaps after fifteen years into the profession they will begin to realize substantial financial gains. In the pastoral ministry, however, except for those rare pastors who serve up to forty years in the same congregation, whenever a move occurs, there is a new community to be introduced to, new client base, new skills to be learned, and new costs to be amortized. For the pastor these seem to be on never-ending cycles, whether brief ones of three to four years or ten- or fifteen-year ones throughout a forty-year career. Pastors need to know that these disparities are not indicative of failure to perform adequately in ministry. It is simply that the other professions are on a different economic track.

For the pastor, the servant role constitutes the call. The cost of that servant role may be far more in evidence twenty or thirty years into the ministry than in the first two or three. In our survey the three factors that were pinpointed as the most significant disadvantages of ministry were lack of privacy, financial stress, and twenty-four-hour duty. Those three factors alone can wear a pastor down, and are burdens that peer professions over a long period of time can adjust schedules and lifestyles to avoid. These disadvantages were reported by both new and experienced pastors. One can handle stress from these three sources when one truly understands that pastoring as a spiritual calling is "the sure foundation" at the core of one's ministry.

Of the nine factors pastors were asked to indicate as problems for their families, the top two problematic areas were inadequate income and lack of personal friends. As just noted, inadequate income will always be a factor in ministry, but perhaps more serious is the lack of personal friends. Some of this may be attributed to the fact that pastors, perhaps correctly, believe they cannot develop close personal friendships within the congregation. A deeper problem suggests that pastors tend to be competitive enough with one another that, unlike business professionals who find time to develop strong bonds with peers over vacations, joint ventures, and peer reviews, pastors as a group continue to be somewhat individualistic. Therefore, they feel even more alienated and have even less support than they might like or need. They tend to believe that support from the congregation is not strong nor do they find much support from other pastors. There seems to be little opportunity for pastors to let down their hair, minister to each other, and otherwise to talk with other pastors about their real needs and concerns.

More than financial restrictions and the lack of personal friends is the third highest-ranking problem for the pastor's family in our survey: inadequate time with one's family. While the centrality of call is most important, supportive activities with family and friends are critical for the pastor to be able to minister over a long period of time.

Guiding the Call

In the movement from call to pulpit one encounters search committees, fellow pastors, ordination committees, and supervising elders (pastors, bishops, association and presbytery executives, synod officers) who are available and responsible to help guide the pastor's call. Bishops, presbytery and synod executives, and contracts are other forms by which the church helps to guide the pastor from call to pulpit. Inattentiveness to these guidelines by supervisors or due process can only provoke discouragement and disaster for the pastor. Any minister's call needs guidance. Much of that can be accomplished through informal means, but some of it must be done through formal procedures including contractual agreements.

For those who have not grown up within a professional family, the pastoral ministry like any other profession may become idealized to the point of distortion. Every profession has its duties and obligations that are far from glamorous and never appear in recruiting brochures. For example, the physician may have to leave a birthday dinner to take an emergency call. The attorney may have to appear in court when he or she had promised the family a long-delayed vacation. The corporate jet pilot is going to have to make coffee, sweep the carpet, and clean out sick bags. The minister will have to keep tabs on the janitor and the thermostat and fight with the manse committee over faulty equipment. These need not damage or curtail motivational events. But they are aspects of the call in which peers, elders, and the formal mechanisms could give guidance to young pastors as they move from enthusiastic call to serious, effective pastoring.

Unlike some of the glamour professions, pay is not everything for the minister. From our survey we hypothesize that if bishops and synod officers distance themselves from the fledgling pastor, the more likely the financial package will become prominent. In the glamour professions agents, attorneys, and others handle fees, salaries, and negotiations for clients. In these professions the measure of one's worth becomes quickly translated into the tangibles of salary. However, in the ministry the more one is willing to trust human guidance of one's call, the less significant and prickly become issues of finances and salary. We conclude that one's ministry will be more effective when the payoff is viewed in terms other than money.

Small-Print Warnings

The fine-print warnings for the ministry become focused primarily on the problem of becoming overextended, putting in jeopardy one's own mental, spiritual, and emotional health as well as one's neglect of the important gift of family and friends. An American Baptist minister observes:

> There was real tension over the time I gave to church obligations and to family obligations. Also, my wife and I got too involved in the church.

A Church of God pastor chants the same litany:

There was tremendous emotional drain with no time for the family.

An Episcopal priest summarizes it well:

There was a marital triangle between church, spouse, and me.

A Lutheran pastor observes:

At different stages in our family life, the workload and hours away were especially stressful. Nights were particularly difficult. It was more so in the early years because we had only one car.

A small-print warning pertains to the pastor's own need for attentiveness to spiritual discipline. Failure to find time for renewal and update of the call from God results in one's ministry quickly becoming like the seed that falls on rocky ground.

In sum, respondents to our survey saw three universal advantages and disadvantages in ministry. The disadvantages of lack of privacy, twenty-four-hour availability, and financial stress come with the territory. The advantages of creative work, flexible schedule, and support of the congregation are counterbalancing. But a firm spiritual commitment to ministry, a commitment by the entire family, holds the advantages and disadvantages in creative tension.

Significant shifts may occur in the clergy or clergy family's sense of vocational certainty. If the disadvantages begin to pile up and the advantages seem to slip away, the pastor and family will experience sharply elevated levels of stress and conflict. Should the pastor continue in ministry? Or, under these circumstances, would continuing put the spiritual welfare of the pastoral family and the congregation at risk? If ministry and marriage are to endure, it is essential that clergy adjust to changes in the family and in ministry in such a way that one's sense of the value of advantages is renewed and the burden of disadvantages placed in perspective.

5

Exemplars of Ministry

All Christians are called to live exemplary lives that are based upon the life and teachings of Christ as adopted by the specific faith communities to which they belong. At a theological level the Christian community claims that all are called to the same standard of moral conduct and Christian witness. However, at the practical level most laypeople look toward the professional or ordained ministry as Christians who are singled out by their status to live out that exemplary life. Because they are ordained to full-time Christian ministry, the clergy also feel pressured to live out faithfully and consistently the official teachings and doctrines of the church. Pastors sense that they are under greater moral and social scrutiny than the laity are. In part this assessment is true because ordination implies that "taking the yoke of obedience includes the representative role in total life. The ordained minister is not asked to lead a different moral life from lay Christians, but he or she is expected to live a life that is 'officially' representative of the total ministry of the church."[1]

Because the community of faith calls the pastor to be its official representative, the clergy find themselves in a double bind. At a practical level, they are expected to be moral examples of high Christian living and, unlike the laity, they are also called to a formal and official accountability to the Christian community. This essentially contractual agreement implies that for the clergy no official spiritual difference exists between the life lived while "on duty" and one's private life.

In discussions about accountability, clergy and laity are

uncomfortable with legalistic language used to regulate and judge the clergy's life. However, some acceptable standard of accountability must be set forth. The difficulty in doing this is in the nature of standards, which must be measured against a norm. Does the observable behavior conform to the stated norms of the congregation and the faith community? Regardless, how are observers to measure the inner, spiritual, motivational life? The problem is humorously illustrated by comedian Bill Cosby. In one of his talks, he mentions "the weapon," which as a forty-nine-year-old male he learned from his grandfather and father. They taught him to ignore his wife's calling him to a task, to dinner, or to errands she wants him to run. The "weapon" resides in the *interior* life of the unresponsive husband: "She can't *prove* that you didn't hear her call."

True, a congregation cannot prove that a pastor is unspiritual, immoral in thought, or complacent in intention to serve the Gospel. Those rubrics that call the pastor to accountability may in the final analysis seem unfair to the pastor. The pastor can, however, hide in his/her passive aggressiveness by not answering the congregation's call to accountability.

In our study, comments over stress and pressures felt by the minister suggested two different groupings. A higher percentage of those clergy whose families of origin were professionals, regardless of the size of towns or cities from which they came, responded that the pressures were about as expected. By contrast, those clergy who came from working-class or blue-collar families and whose families lived in population centers of 50,000 or less (sixty-four percent of respondents) characteristically expressed the belief that pressures on both the clergy and family members, especially spouses, were higher than expected. These respondents also commented about excessive pressures and double standards: the *clergy* family was to be exemplary in moral conduct and in church and civic activities. From these two groups one surmises that in the socialization process of a professional family, the clergy have somehow integrated the objective standards of behavior with personal, private, subjective experiences. But those who come from a working class tend to associate work with the times that one is "on clock" while they regard one's private, personal life as "off clock."

One PCUSA pastor complains:

I consider the lack of time with family because of all the "work-week-plus" demands on my time to be a problem. I include my two children in this.

Responses to our survey show that working-class families in larger population centers are socially more sophisticated than those from small-town or rural settings. Thus, a pastor who comes from a working-class family living in a city of over 50,000 is better able to adjust to clergy pressures. We conclude that the more sophisticated social environment of a town of that size makes it easier for both professional and working-class families to accommodate themselves to complex cultural expectations. We see little difference between the two groups when they come from communities of 50,000 or more.

The dilemma for the pastor as an exemplar of ministry is that the pastor and the pastor's family are called to fulfill the letter and the spirit of the law of Christ as well as the expectations that the local church held when it called the pastor. Bill Cosby can make people laugh over his wife's frustrations when he chooses not to hear her call, but in actual life the minister cannot take refuge in refusing to hear the call to accountability whether to marriage, to a local congregation, or to a denomination. It is spiritually fallacious for the pastor to retreat into a subjective spirituality that refuses to be accountable to the contractual terms under which the pastor has agreed to work with a congregation.

A Nazarene pastor reflects on the pain:

It is hard to juggle ministry responsibilities and opportunities with family [obligations].

Terms of Call

Each pastor serving a congregation is bound to a standard of accountability. The specifics of that accountability are more explicitly stated in call-oriented churches such as the Baptist, Presbyterian, Lutheran and Assemblies of God. Contractual agreements are also implied for clergy from denominations whose bishops or other officials appoint pastors to congregations such as the United Methodist Church. In the call-oriented church, the terms of the contract may be specifically tailored to needs of that congregation. In the appointment system, the terms may be more general, but any preliminary discussions, interviews, or assessments concerning matching the clergy person with the congregation—whether formally stated or not—constitute a contractual agreement with the clergy to perform certain services and meet certain needs within that local church and parish.

The initial meeting of a prospective pastor and a church committee is actually a negotiating session. The congregational representatives, whether gathered at an informal social setting to chat with the prospect or engaged in formal, no-nonsense contract deliberations, are endeavoring to set the terms of pastoral employment. For them the talks have a psychologically binding quality. The uninitiated pastor, on the other hand, may mistakenly think of the discussions as merely a get-acquainted time and not realize that they are about binding agreements concerning the conduct of ministry. The pastor may offer no more than a polite nod of the head that signals agreement to key areas of ministerial commitment. An important shift has occurred: the general agenda topics for ministry become binding agreements as far as the congregation is concerned though perhaps they have not in the mind of the pastor.

Pastors in a call system understand the specific forms of accountability to the local congregation perhaps more clearly and precisely than appointed clergy. In both instances the clergy is a representative of the community of faith. But in a call system the clergy will identify the community of faith primarily with a specific congregation because that particular group called and perhaps ordained the pastor. Those pastors who serve under an appointive system and whose credentials are not held by a local congregation may mistakenly not see themselves as accountable to the local congregation's needs. In both cases, however, through example and leadership the pastor is expected to provide a spiritual ministry that meets the needs of the local congregation and that is consistent with the teachings and doctrines of the larger community of faith of which any Christian congregation is a part.

In our study, the clergy comments and responses to personal and family pressure have less to do with unrealistic denominational expectations than with specific conflicts within the local congregation. An Episcopal rector reflects on this conflict and his naïveté:

> I was called to a congregation that wanted to be cleaned and shaped up. I naïvely believed them.

Two sets of legal terminology may help us at this point. Those who hold corporate responsibilities such as chief executive officers and directors of boards or corporations (profit and non-profit alike) have both a personal fiduciary (good faith) relationship and a corporate fiduciary relationship in the discharge of their responsibilities. Strictly speaking, the pastor may not incur the precise set of obligations that a member of the board of directors or the president of IBM, Boeing, or McDonalds does because these positions have externally imposed obligations. The notion of a fiduciary obligation in management roles does not readily translate into specific legal requirements for pastoral functions. However, the terms are helpful in assisting clergy to a better understanding of the complexity of a congregation's expectation and the pastor's agreement to serve.

The fiduciary relationship in effect says that the clergy has an obligation to act in good faith in the pastoral care of the parish. This implies that he/she has a responsibility to act with acceptable intentions, to be wise and prudent in the discharge of pastoral functions for those within the church. As long as the pastor demonstrates intentions to fulfill the expectations of the call, any falling short of those intentions is probably minimized. That is, some failures or poor results are not a consequence of the pastor's acting in bad faith. Many church-life failures can be attributed to economic downturn, moral scandal within the congregation, or the inability of the pastor despite his/her intentions to be a good evangelist or pulpiteer. As long as the pastor exhibits intentions to fulfill the "good faith" commitment to the congregation, the pastor in effect has discharged to a satisfactory level the obligation to the congregation.

By contrast corporate fiduciary relationship stipulates that the pastor has certain obligations due to status and loyalty to the corporation. So, for example, an Episcopal priest assumes a corporate fiduciary relation to the denomination to provide the Sacrament of the Lord's Supper on a weekly basis. United Methodists will probably remain in good standing if they administer the Sacrament only quarterly. Other denominations may not have a requirement to celebrate the Lord's Supper at all. Likewise, a Baptist pastor has a corporate fiduciary responsibility to baptize by immersion; while in Methodist communions the candidate for baptism may choose between immersion and sprinkling.

On noncontroversial tenets of faith, a pastor will probably experience little conflict in efforts to meet tests of loyalty to denominational standards. Where theological conflict exists between the denominational standards or constitution and local churches or clergy, the theological obligation of a corporate fiduciary relationship is subject to rigorous dispute. For example, to demonstrates loyalty to the Southern Baptist Convention, all SBC pastors must embrace a specific biblical hermeneutic. By the same token, this appeal to a universal nonvariant standard makes the SBC a *confessional* church, which is gallingly contrary to Convention standards and tradition.

Of course, the observant reader will note that indiscriminate and absolute clergy obedience to preexisting denominational practices and standards muzzles the prophetic voice and may well place the pastor in a conflict between allegiance to denominational standards and expectations and the obligation to provide satisfactory pastoral care in the congregation. Any charges of heresy or spiritual failure on the pastor's part will cause additional conflict and place fiduciary strain upon both the local congregation and the national ecclesial body.

When a pastor is ordained, he/she accepts both the challenge of a good-faith relationship to a congregation and the loyalty relationship to the denomination. In a United Methodist congregation, one can assume that the pastor has a corporate obligation not to use alcohol in the celebration of the Lord's Supper because the *Discipline* calls for the use of unfermented juice. But in the Episcopal and Lutheran churches, ecclesial obligation may in fact direct use of wine in the Sacrament and perhaps wine of a certain alcoholic content.

Regardless of a pastor's personal theological stance, the denomination has a corporate obligation to the minister in accordance with its stated and accepted practices. A pastor may fulfill all corporate obligations but still be criticized, called to accountability, and dismissed because the congregation judges its pastor to have failed in his or her fiduciary relation to provide reasonable, agreed-upon care to the church. A congregation may amass evidence to demonstrate to denominational officials that while the pastor fulfilled corporate obligations, the pastor served the local church ineffectively and failed to act in good faith.

A call to pastor a church presumes both a fiduciary relation to the congregation and a corporate fiduciary relation to the denominational body. At times these responsibilities are in conflict. One may fulfill the expectations of one set of fiduciary relationships while failing to meet the stipulations inherent in the other. The minister is never entirely free to act on his/her personal agenda. As pastor, one is called into a community of faith but must always live with the realization that the larger community has a spiritual wisdom that transcends the pastor's personal faith perspective. The pastor knows that as an exemplar of ministry, his/her family also contributes to the well-being of that community.

Called to Accountability

Being a minister and receiving affirmation as a good pastor involves far more than simply being a good and likable Christian. As an exemplar of ministry the pastor is called to a quality of Christian living that transcends one's personal, subjective feelings. Constructive theology draws its power from words and phrases like "grace," "forgiveness," "acceptance," "servant," and "bearing one another's burdens"; therefore, concepts of loyalty, standards, obligations, and accountability do not surface readily without the connotations of law, legalism, works righteousness, etc. Consequently, we now turn to the language of the legal system in which the terminology of agreement, contract, obligation, and adversary are the everyday language, and where they do not carry the negative theological associations that weigh them down when associated with ministry.

When one applies the analogy of the legal process to the ministry to explain principles of accountability, several concerns immediately present themselves. The central problem is identified by Thomas A. Robinson:

> The legal system starts from an adversarial viewpoint. That is to say that our legal framework assumes that everyone's interests are best served when placed in a context of power and conflict. This

"us versus them syndrome" can be dangerous from a theological standpoint. Similarly, much of the tort litigation may be centered around the issue of victimization and it may be that our faith calls us to a different experience.[2]

Pastors are called to be exemplars of ministry and not to the role of adversary of the denomination or the local congregation. Besides, an adversarial position is not inherent in a call to ministry. The typical minister has a penchant for avoiding overtly adversarial roles; therefore, the issue of accountability becomes even more difficult and emotionally heavy laden. But accountability cannot be ignored simply because it is resisted. The vast percentage of negative comments in our survey result from pastors failing to understand or fulfill their fiduciary responsibility to their congregations.

The pastor's responsibilities inevitably lead into some dimension of power, conflict, and adversative relations. The conflicts may not be adversarial in the sense of the legal system, but theologically they can be in the sense that Moses and Aaron were in conflict with the people of Israel as they led them out of Egypt. God's decision to choose Israel as his own people and to display his gracious nature through them placed him at odds with the Egyptian government.

In the New Testament context, immediately following Peter's great Christological confession of Matthew 16:23, Jesus has to say harshly to Peter, "Get behind me, Satan!" Also, the pastoral letters of St. Paul were written to settle the conflict over theological positions and their ecclesial power. The apostle often found himself in an adversarial position both with factions within the New Testament churches as he contended for faithful adherence to the Gospel and with the church as a whole in Galatia, Corinth, and Rome.

It is important to understand that these conflicts and adversarial relationships can be overcome. The pastors surveyed were often naïve about the level of tension that exists in pastoring. Pastors may complain that pressure is put on them. For example a Church of God pastor wrote:

> [Our] marital problems were caused by unrealistic, self-inflicted stress on my wife, and led to alienation and an interest in getting out of the ministry.

A PCUSA pastor says:

People expect you to be almost everywhere all the time. Everyone wants to be served.

But one must ask about causes of this terrible pressure and consider whether it is self-imposed. Is it a failure to fulfill fiduciary responsibilities? Has the pastor in some way neglected or forgotten that corporate fiduciary relations may help to ease local church leadership tensions? In ordination one agrees to a contract with the Gospel, and in the covenant of ordination the pastor agrees to perform certain activities for the congregation and the denomination.

The challenge of the Gospel and ordination is to integrate the so-called fiduciary (general care) and corporate fiduciary (denominational) responsibility in grace-filled ways that transcend and transform implied legalisms. For example, Jesus' Sermon on the Mount and his teachings (especially parables) and indeed his entire ministry (including his death and resurrection) established the radical nature of the Incarnation: Jesus came not to *enforce* the law with the heavy hand of a prophet, priest, or king, but to transform it by promulgating a new law, "the royal law" of love. This means that any legalistic denotations of the contractual agreements in ordination are to be transformed by a higher calling and a higher authority. Let us put this theological truth into the context of our discussion: The theology of ordination calls the pastor to transcend any legalistic stance that *forces* him or her to prove that he/she has fulfilled the contract. Rather, in theological terms, the pastor, as an exemplar of ministry, should boast, "The burden of proof rests on me."[3]

This is not a defensive posture but a positive motivation. Paraphrased, this theological principle encourages the pastor to claim, "My standard of pastoral conduct should be such that I bear the burden of proof by going the second mile, giving the cloak off my back, binding up the wounds of others, fulfilling all righteousness both in the letter and spirit of the law." If clergy can move toward this positive motivation, they could at least begin to address many of their comments about the hurts, physical illnesses, family pressures, rebellious children, discontentment with ministry, and severe personal depression.

The legal system assumes that through testimony and cross-examination truth will emerge. In ministry the truth of spiritual performance cannot be ascertained by these means. The truth of the Cross will displayed, in the final analysis, through radical commitment to Jesus Christ and by one's bearing witness to that radicality, not through direct cross-examination and ministerial performance. Nonetheless, pastors want the truth to be manifest that their congregations appreciate what they do in the discharge of their fiduciary obligations, and that their families are not treated unfairly either by themselves or by the churches they serve, and that their families are not held to higher standards of social, economic, and spiritual accountability than other laypeople.

These are difficult issues to adjudicate, principally because ministry and Christian life are based upon the positive motivation to become exemplars of the life and call of Jesus Christ. But if pastors are able to place their personal lives and leadership responsibilities in the context of this positive theological motivation, problem resolution can be clearly and positively realized and effectively lived out. In the following sections we endeavor to suggest how a variety of clergy fiduciary relationships can be placed in such a context.

Stating the Case

From our study we have identified seven aspects of ministerial leadership that are important for clergy to understand if they are to develop a reasonable, loving model for accountability.

Terms of the Call. When a pastor moves to a congregation, conditions of the call are both explicit and implied. These conditions relate to challenges of ministry, possible new prophetic ministries, needs of the congregation, and the pastor's strengths. The more specific, open, and mutually agreed upon the terms of a call are, the easier the adjustment for both congregation and pastor.

Pastor Open to Scrutiny. The pastor is an exemplar of ministry and therefore both conduct, intention, and his/her behavior with church and family will be subject to scrutiny. The congregation and the secular community will make judgments and assessments about the personal and corporate fiduciary obligations of the pastor. In this sense the pastor is an elected official like a mayor, county commissioner, or city council member. The pastor is a public figure, and his/her comings and goings will always be open to closer scrutiny than those of the general population. In 2 Kings, for example, the prophet Nathan had to remind David that his role as commander-in-chief of the Israelite army carried with it a corporate fiduciary responsibility not to manipulate the battle so that he, David, would gain unfair advantage.

Unresolved Conflict. Discrepancies will always exist between the congregation and the pastor in their understanding of what terms of the call imply and what the pastor is called to do. Some aspects of those conflicts will never go away. If one conflict is resolved, in all likelihood another will surface. There will be friction, disparity, and tension between the pastor's view of what ministry means and the congregation's. Neither pastor nor congregation, regardless of how loving or spiritual either may be, can make all of this confusion disappear. The pastor must learn to analyze and process the conflicts and not take them as defeats. One need look only at the Pastoral Epistles to understand that some of the most creative pastoral leadership resulted from efforts to resolve spiritual conflicts.

Accountability As a Form of Due Process. To engage in reviews, to appear before committees, boards, commissions, or a group of clergy peers does not have to be a negative experience. This is simply a part of the due process of ministry. Participation in a spiritual retreat, a day of reflection, or church planning is part of due process. The concept of due process means that not everyone is going to be happy. When a conflict and its causes are reviewed, each party enters into the due process negotiation with some degree of assumption that it is right and will win. If a party doesn't think it has a case, it wouldn't raise the issue. Any time a dispute emerges, either party has a 50/50 chance to win. That is due process, an opportunity to process the dispute, not a guarantee of victory.

Picky Specifics. Often the issues that rise in a dispute are not central to that conflict. Specific examples of unacceptable performance or behavior may be cited because they can be isolated from other forms of behavior and identified in an uncomplicated way as areas of concern. Yet specifics do not tell the whole story of ministry. The question of whether the pastor put in a full work week and how that is defined or whether the pastor filled out appropriate paperwork for denominational purposes or filed proper marriage and baptismal certificates are specifics that may be legitimate concerns calling for the review process. But sometimes undue attention may be focused upon a particular set of circumstances or performance expectations as an indirect and often unconscious way of criticizing the pastor or of trying to motivate the pastor to be more sensitive or responsible in another area of ministry. The laity may need help to focus on the real problem that requires resolution.

Lost in the Translation. Whenever a pastor is required to give an explanation for days off or for having taken excessive vacation time, or to give reasons for seeking continuing education— whenever the pastor has to make any kind of defensive statement—something will always be lost in the translation. There will always be aspects of the problem under scrutiny that will not be addressed and will be omitted from discussion. The pastor simply has to accept the fact that not everything that might be said from either side can, will, or should be said.

Family Stress. Because a pastor is a public figure and the pastor's faithfulness to the terms of call to a parish will gain notoriety, the parsonage family will feel the stress rising from any discussions between the congregation and the pastor regarding that faithfulness. The pastor can never make stress on the family go away because the boundaries between private and public or professional life are not clear-cut and the performance of ministry will always be open to view. At the same time, the congregation's evaluation of the pastor will be influenced by the attitudes and behavior of the family.

Examining and Negotiating the Realities

Issues of Responsibility. In our survey we identified eight pastoral responsibilities that are crucial for effective ministry if the pastor is to meet the fiduciary expectations of the congregation. These activities also are the sources of greatest stress to the pastor. Each pastoral care responsibility should be openly negotiated by the pastor with lay leadership, if exemplary ministry by pastor and church is to be realized.

The pastors ranked creative work and a flexible schedule as the two greatest advantages to being a minister. Inherent in these advantages lurk problems for the unsuspecting pastor. There is no easy way to define "creative work" or to ascribe productivity and high level of performance or expectation to a flexible work schedule. The same pastors reported that the most significant disadvantage to being a minister is being on call twenty-four hours a day. This is followed by lack of privacy. Concerns such as living in a church-owned home and pressure on the children to be "perfect" ranked lower than one might expect. The highest level of conflict occurs between the pastor's high value placed upon creativity and flexibility and congregational expectations of the pastor's availablility any time of the day and night. This conflict is the focus of the eight basic pastoral tasks discussed next.

Preaching Ministry. The centrality of the preaching ministry is exemplified in pulpit committees or search committees of call-oriented churches. Preaching has historically been considered central to the task of ministry and to the vitality of the congregation. Pastors have a responsibility to preach and to put substantial time into preparation to do so. At the same time the congregation understands that not all pastors are equally gifted as public speakers. The laity are concerned that the pastor give a fair account of himself or herself in the pulpit and not dismiss this essential corporate theological responsibility as "something I'm not good at doing." A primary emphasis placed upon preaching by laity should surprise no minister. A pastor who expects to excel in ministry but hates preaching is like an airline pilot who has a morbid fear of flying. Those who have a fear of preaching and leading worship should consider other than local-church forms of ministry.

Youth Ministry. Each congregation should understand that the vitality of its future and its ability to attract couples with children depend to a singular degree upon having some type of youth ministry and a strong Christian education program. Sustained efforts to reach out to youth and to confront them with Jesus Christ are essential. Youth are delightful yet fickle and rebellious, living in a constant state of personal and educational transition. They require continual cultivation, but no pastor or church can afford to make youth ministry its single focus. Both youth and parents can appreciate the risks involved when a pastor overidentifies with the youth and neglects other aspects of ministry. The pastor has a responsibility to negotiate a commitment to a strong youth ministry while at the same time recognizing the needs of the total church.

Pastoral Visitation. Congregations may place too much value on pastoral visitation in the home and overestimate its effectiveness, but a universal complaint against pastors is their failure to do enough home visitation. Not surprisingly, pastors report that visitation is their most difficult task. Many believe it's a waste of time and that people don't want a pastor invading their privacy. In the last decade the phenomenal increase of small-group ministry, which often takes place in homes, probably is a partial response to people's wanting the personal contact of ministry in their homes. Both pastoral visiting and church small-group ministry are ways to build up the church, sharing needs, and gaining and offering personal concern as ministry.

Many pastors are unable to understand that their own needs as ministers can well be served as they visit from house to house. They must be willing to do home visitation not just to secure funds for a budget, buttonhole people for church jobs, or poke around looking for family crises where none may exist. Rather, the larger dimension of home visitation is one of nurturing the body of Christ, learning who people are and how they live within their home environment. Home visitation is probably the most positive but the most often neglected aspect of ministry.

Crisis Intervention. Members of the congregation want pastors to intervene in times of crisis. Sometimes the intervention expectation is unrealistic because people also want the pastor to perform miracles of healing of body, family, and personal wounds that can come only through the grace of God in Christ. Pastors must develop skills of crisis intervention, whether praying for people in medically critical situations, ministering to a family after an unexpected death, consoling a spouse whose mate has just left, or working cooperatively with mental health and law officials to intervene in matters of physical, sexual, and drug abuse. The pastor must minister in crises where spiritual and emotional alienation occurs even though distressed parishioners frequently overestimate the serious consequences and the pastor is not a magician. At the same time, if the pastor is not prepared and skilled in crisis ministry, the pastor will inevitably inflame the situation by overreacting.

Budget Raising. Often those who have leadership responsibilities for charitable organizations are selected because they have a certain expertise. Pastors, by the same logic, are criticized for spending money but not raising it. One of the concerns that require delicate and definite clarity is the pastor's fiscal responsibility to the church. How much control over budget items does the pastor have? What about raising the budget? Congregations with members from the financial community such as bankers, financial consultants, and small-business owners can better understand that pastors are not professional fund raisers. Laity should carry the bulk of responsibility for the church budget; however, the pastor is remiss if he or she tries to avoid responsibility in this area of church life, and some congregations may expect the pastor to bear significant responsibility for that area of church life. Again, a congregation may be overly optimistic about its financial ability to engage in a specific type of ministry, or perhaps the pastor has not been upfront about the actual costs of a pet project. Also, the pastor must make financial contributions to the church.

Pastoral Reports. Most denominations require some type of periodic reporting. Such terse accountability is not undue punishment, but the pastor must expend a great deal of energy to make reports more creative than simply to rehearse the bare bones of dry statistics. Laity are interested in what the pastor does, and they need to be reminded in creative and entertaining ways of the various aspects of pastoral ministry that may escape proper recognition and assessment. Lacking these periodic reports, neither the pastor nor the congregation can appreciate the work, creativity, and forms of ministry that are carried out routinely.

Because pastoral ministry involves many unscheduled events, a pastor may be tempted to hide behind or to become overwhelmed by the variety of pastoral tasks. When report time is due, the endless hours and energy seem to fade into statistical insignificance. The pastor's conflict between the advantage of a flexible and creative work schedule and the endless intrusive demands of ministry will reemerge. As a matter of personal and spiritual self-discipline, the pastor should keep a diary of activities to remind both church members and himself/herself how time has been invested.

Visitation of the Homebound. Developing a ministry to the homebound is an essential responsibility for the pastor, and the one who has an effective homebound ministry is engaged in one of the important tasks of pastoral leadership. Every congregation, even young, rapidly growing suburban congregations, includes elderly people. Also, we are seeing more parents and grandparents living with children, even if only temporarily while, for instance, recovering from illness. And of course included in the homebound may very likely be younger adults as well as children.

Whether or not openly acknowledged, everyone fears being neglected and forgotten. And people who are confined to home, regardless of the reason, become acutely sensitive to their finitude and appreciate pastoral care. In visitation of the homebound, the pastor also sets an example for the laity, exhibiting love and care without awkwardness or timidity in the face of serious injuries, debilitating illness, and approaching death. By taking the initiative in this area, the pastor is truly an exemplar of ministry.

Some parishioners have an insatiable need to receive care, to feel spiritual and emotional reassurance and comfort, and the pastor who regularly calls upon the homebound during the normal workday receives fewer phone calls and intrusions during family time at the parsonage. By making routine visits to the homebound, the pastor can effectively eliminate much of the oppression experienced from being on call twenty-four hours a day.

Nurture and Congregational Growth. Whether or not a congregation is located in an area blessed with great potential for membership growth, one indication of positive church life is an increase in the number of people participating in various church activities. The pastor may be a great preacher and a great home visitor, and the congregation may believe it has statistics to prove remarkable growth. But true spiritual growth is far more complex than statistical advances in giving and attendance because true growth is qualitative as well as quantitative. The pastor must make a significant commitment to nurture the spirituality of the body of Christ. If the pastor is able both to care for and nurture the church *while encouraging members to care and nurture each other,* spiritual life of the church will be healthier and complaints minimal.

We suggest that pastoral ministry carries with it a commitment to assume responsibility for these eight basic pastoral tasks. The conflict between the pastor and the congregation over whether the pastor is doing a satisfactory job, we believe, is related to either success or failure in addressing each of the areas of pastoral responsibility discussed above. Be advised, however, that no pastor or congregation is equally strong in all eight areas. But the eight responsibilities must be seen as significant areas of ministry to which both pastor and people must commit themselves. We suggest that when concentrated, prayerful commitment to these eight areas occurs, both the congregation and pastor will perceive themselves as exemplars of ministry.

Issues of Covenant and Contract. When a pastor or church believes it has been injured in a previous working relationship, the temptation rises to make the working relationship primarily a contractual arrangement, in an effort to protect against reinjury. We offer several guidelines to maximize advantages and minimize disadvantages of the mutual expectations of pastor and congregation.

1. Written contracts should cover the basic guidelines but should not be so extensive or so restrictive that either party thinks the agreement includes every possible area of conflict. In theological terms, a pastoral relationship is built upon a covenant. It may use some contractual language, but in the last analysis it is a faith covenant between a pastor and a congregation. The reason mutual expectations must be explicit is to encourage each party to articulate what it wants to give and receive. This is both an appropriate and a fair spiritual exercise. Some type of written covenant, job description, or contract is essential if a good, healthful relationship between pastor and congregation is to form.

2. Some kind of explicit agreement about anticipated growth either in numbers or quality of nurture within the congregation must be worked into the contractual arrangement. One of the classic conflicts between pastors and lay leaders occurs as a result of the difference in training and vocation. The pastor is skilled in study, education, nurture, and pastoral care. Many aspects of these skills would be considered by financial and

business leaders as "non-productive"—nice to have for human relations but a questionable productivity asset. Many laity who serve on the session, the board of deacons, the vestry, the administrative board, or whatever are trained in business or finance. They function in a world in which one's performance can be quantified by the often-mentioned "bottom-line criterion." If a pastor agrees to a certain level or quality of growth of a congregation, the pastor had better be able to deliver "the numbers." If the guaranteed numbers relate to an improved quality of pastoral service, the laypeople expect assurances that they will be able to identify and verify ways in which the quality of their spiritual life is increased.

The goal may be to increase the quality of pastoral care or add to the number of people who participate in a variety of church activities. Both parties need to be clear about where the emphasis lies and understand which party is more likely to be affected by a disagreement. If contractual agreements are clear, the danger of protracted disagreements down the road can be avoided.

3. Use of time can be a source of conflict. The classic problem is the pastor's commitment to a weekend-work world. In most business arrangements, either a stipulated shift time, "comp" time, or a rotating on-call schedule for weekend clinics can be scheduled well in advance. Congregations expect its pastoral staff, in a multiple staff situation also, to be present for all the services on Sunday. A plan to rotate staff responsibility for and attendance at particular Sunday services does not work well in a church situation. The logic of work and leisure that occupies the minds of laypeople does not apply to their expectations of the pastor's weekend schedule.

This conflict translates into the need to establish a carefully protected schedule of days off, blocks of time off, and a reasonable expectation of total work hours. If a rationale is not established and supported from the beginning, resentment quickly grows. Laypeople in charge of supervising the pastor will think he/she is shirking responsibilities; and the pastor will conclude that he/she is not appreciated or the amount of hours given to the work recognized.

4. A pastor may have specific family needs such as aging parents nearby, a handicapped child, or of continuing education or a desire to pursue an advanced degree. If these time-

consuming matters are part of the pastor's agenda up front, all can agree on how time will be allocated.

5. Both the congregational representatives and the pastor need to have a meeting of the minds upon mutually declared goals and agenda. If the first three elements mentioned above are constructively negotiated, the goals and agenda will emerge more smoothly and quickly. Both congregation and pastor have their strengths and weaknesses and want to be mutually served so that strengths can be maximized and the weaknesses modified by the strengths. A successful negotiation of a call to a congregation stresses mutual forms of ministry. The discussions may be enlightening and liberating for both parties as they learn to grapple with their mutual vulnerability, embarrassment, and problems of trust. A carefully crafted working relationship will be evidenced in the ways in which the congregation and pastor mutually support each other.

In summary, neither the congregation nor the pastor wants to become involved in negative, contract arbitration. That is inimical to the ministry and spiritually destructive. Distrust raises mutual antagonisms and resentments that can never be worked out. The Gospel calls us to a higher level of trust than is evidenced in the contract negotiations between labor and management or between sports heroes and club owners or entertainment celebrities and production studios.

A basic working agreement (covenant/contract), commitment to the quality of growth and agreement about the broad use of time and to mutually declared goals and agenda, is essential for a healthful working relationship. Legalism obtrudes where the working relationship was too loosely constructed and each party projected onto the other expectations that were not understood and would not have been offered. The goal is to make general, mutual expectations explicit. The result will be a working relationship that achieves those ends.

Our findings suggest that the solution to the problem of family pressures is not so much to lower work expectations or agree to fewer work hours, but to discuss openly and agree upon and support expectations for ministry.

Living With the Consequences

An All Too Human and Spiritual Community. In a highly conflicted or adversarial relationship between a congregation and a pastor, three possibilities for unfairness exist for the clergy that do not exist in the civil legal system.

First, there are no real checks and balances in the clergy system. Official denominational efforts for a fair appeal may exist on paper, but the checks and balances familiar to governmental bodies are not replicated in the church. Therefore, justice is never so easy to come by in the church system as it is in the civil system. Essentially, the church operates on the basis of trust. Therefore, a church-trial system does not provide for appeals because it is not based on a conflictual or adversative relationship.

Second, civil law guarantees four levels by which the truth of one's claim in court can be judged. The first is the right to a trial; the second the right of the losing party to appeal to an intermediate state or federal court; the third is the right to appeal to a state court of appeals and if necessary, because a matter of law has not been honored in a lower court, to a state supreme court; the fourth is the right to appeal to the United States Supreme Court in matters that directly affect the federal government's legal jurisdiction.

Third, juries and judges make mistakes. No one, whether in a civil court system or in a church judicial system, is blessed with infallible judgment. That is why the right of appeal exists in the civil court system.

These three areas of difficulty make mutual accountability, from a legalistic or adversarial position, much more cumbersome and difficult. In the final analysis, no way exists to guarantee that the truth will be heard, that fairness will come in full measure, and that the pastor and the congregation will have access to a system of appeals.

When the Verdict Comes In. As in the biblical example of Jesus' silence before his accusers, the pastor needs to accept the verdict for better or worse and not whine. Pastors are called to be exemplars of Christ in ministry and are not called to test the reliability or justice of the church legal system. Justice from a human point of view will not always occur either in the civil system or within church life. Some pastors and pastors' families have a naïve and romantic idea that because the church is made up of believers in which agape love is the norm for negotiating conflicts, no one will ever be hurt and justice will always run down as a mighty stream. But the church is not based on a system of justice; it is based on grace, call, and commitment by faith even when injustices, wrongs, and trials come one's way.

Spiritual plea bargaining with a congregation may prevent a high-level conflict. Often issues are not crystal clear, and everyone is served when matters are not pressed to conclusion. Plea bargaining is a concession with the hope that a partial truth will suffice and be binding on both parties. But a certain level of maturity, self-esteem, and admission of guilt on the part of both parties is necessary to make plea bargaining work. The advantage is the avoidance of a long, painful, expensive trial. Yet one needs to remember that it may not be in the pastor's best interest to be publicly judged as right. Always winning is not a goal in ministry.

In almost every instance it will be best to settle matters out of court even though the pastor may not be at fault and feels compelled to prove his innocence. In effect the conflict is brought to a certain point of controversy and then is negotiated to a mutually agreed settlement. Suits tried in civil courts usually end with severance of any formal relationship between the two parties. However, the best verdict in a church relationship may be achieved by settling out of court. This way the pastor and congregation will experience loss of only a minimal amount of effective ministry and be able quickly to get on with their work. Perhaps the pastor can continue in that congregation, or circumstances may dictate that pastor and congregation go their separate ways. But justice under the limitations of human frailty is accomplished as well as possible.

Life and Friends "Outside the Courtroom." Life is larger than the courtroom or any conflict a pastor may have with a congregation. Having been placed in a conflicted relationship, a congregation or pastor may become overly defensive and focus on winning a particular point in a given controversy. One's integrity may be at risk. But both parties need to realize that life exists outside the conflicts of a courtroom setting.

A theological word of admonition is in order. All Christians are members of the body of Christ. Life goes on. The sun will rise the next morning. The grace of God will heal wounds of deed and ego. For example, whether in state or national elections, or in the premier sporting events of the Super Bowl,

World Series, NBA Championships, Wimbledon, World Soccer Cup, etc., conflicts are intense during competition. Each person or team wants to win and often tempers flair as pressures swell.

Contrary to the macho aphorism of the late Vince Lombardi, coach of the Green Bay Packers in their glory years, that "there are no good losers only good winners," life goes on. Moral values cannot be reduced to clichés from the sports world. It is noteworthy that following Lombardi's death, his legendary harassing macho tactics became a legacy that reduced the team to mediocrity. But a gracious loser evidences a capacity to understand, even in the heat of battle and defeat, that life is larger than any conflict through which we pass. Perhaps too many pastors are Vince Lombardi clones: Everything must be black or white! Win or lose! Right or wrong! The belief is that one must maintain total victory to sustain personal integrity. Such is not the life of the Gospel or the church. Grace abounds both during the conflict and following the conflict—for the parties on both sides of the contention.

Be Open to New Guidance and Inspiration. As conflicts resolve themselves, the pastor needs to be open to nurture after the dispute. That nurture may come from peers, family members, people within the congregation, or friends outside the church. Where conflicts occur and verdicts are rendered, one is called to reevaluate one's life and ministry, based as they are now following the disagreement, on the new realities with which one is faced. Such evaluation is not easy, but when self-assessment does not occur, the pastor lapses into fighting old battles and new pressures, making life nearly unbearable for the pastor and his/her family.

From comments offered about pressures on the pastor, our study indicates that reports of the level of conflict and the ways in which they manifest themselves (rebellious children, spouses and children who avoid church activities) generally come from pastors acknowledging their naïveté, spiritual gullibility, and insensitivity to themselves and to the insensitivities, naïveté, and demands of the parish. If pastors will objectively evaluate the work world into which the pastor is called as an exemplar of Christ, the pastor will avoid legalistic or adversarial confrontations with the congregation. And, from our perspective, learning to live with the consequences of being an ordained minister, detailed above, will go a long way toward elimination of many causes of the stress that respondents recite as problems in their ministry.

As difficult as it may seem, a pastor must open himself/herself to new guidance and inspiration after resolution of a dispute. If it doesn't happen, the consequences of that failure exacerbate problems, and one loses the unique opportunity to grow into a new self-awareness and more effective ministry.

6

Healing Clergy Family Conflicts/Injuries

Introduction

The goal of this chapter is to increase the diagnostic skills of the pastor so that he/she learns to identify categories of injury or conflict, determine the seriousness of problems, and administer proper treatment so as to forestall failure in ministry and, in fact, enhance likelihood of effective ministry and healthful clergy family/congregation relations. We will look at various types of conflicts and injuries that occur in a clergy family. This includes the pastor's family of marriage as well as the pastor's spiritual family, the local congregation. We want to examine the problems that create the injuries and conflicts, and offer specific suggestions and guidance for dealing in a positive way with them while at the same time trying to avoid becoming moralistic or too prescriptive. Many books and studies about clergy families and clergy crises focus on a long catalog and long descriptions of the problems. Some may offer extensive analyses of sources of difficulties but fall short of prescribing ways of coping with them.

Without trying to tell people how to run their lives either as clergy or congregation, we offer specific suggestions that rise from our study. Some of the topics discussed from the survey findings are the advantages and disadvantages of ministry, issues concerning vacation time, and family problems.

Types of Injuries

While our primary focus in this chapter is on clergy and clergy family injuries and how to overcome them, we must remember that we are all part of the body of Christ. Therefore, injuries that occur to a clergy or clergy family member also injure the body of Christ, including the local congregation and the entire denomination. Injuries and conflicts are never one-sided. Ministry involves mutuality. Consequently, we address both clergy and congregation. If solutions are not mutually satisfying, that is, if they do not apply in equally constructive ways to the congregation and pastor, the solutions will not work in the long term for either.

Injuries are mutually experienced; healing also has to be mutually experienced. And healing can occur. One way to help a congregation and a pastor overcome their conflicts and injuries is to offer both analysis and remedy. Constructive and well-founded guidelines for the clergy family will be a source of relief of stress, confusion, conflict, and injury to the congregation. Theologically both the congregation and the pastor aspire, in their best moments, to be exemplars individually and corporately of the life, teaching, and ministry offered in Christ. Therefore, a common basis for ministry and for the overcoming of difficulties in ministry is reaffirmed.

For example, if a solution for clergy injuries is more time off, both the congregation and the pastor must recognize it as mutually helpful. It is not a financial drain on the congregation nor should the clergy feel guilty for taking more time. Another example is the pastor who must leave a congregation under duress. Both the congregation and the pastor must see that in a basic and significant way this ministry was a mutually shared failure. During the pastorate, misunderstood expectations, hidden agendas, failure of nerve, radical change of circumstances, or a totally unexpected and disastrous crisis may have served as the precipitator. When a minister and a congregation go separate ways, a pastor divorces, or a rebellious member of the clergy family rejects the church and ministry, the entire family and the congregation suffer the pain. All are called to forgive and accept God's grace in any resulting disillusionment.

Our analysis suggests three major types of conflicts or injuries. In discussing these, our goal goes beyond presenting evidence or offering commentary. Our hope is that this chapter will increase the diagnostic capacities of both clergy and congregations to understand better the injuries and their implications.

Superficial or Obvious Injury

This type of injury is obvious to all but often is ignored. It is dismissed as insignificant; folks conclude that it simply comes with the territory and is not to be taken seriously. Analogously, if one ignores a superficial cut, scratch, low-grade fever, or other chronic complaint, more serious problems often result, or the symptoms point to more serious underlying problems.

Deeper Injuries or Fractures

Deeper wounds may include a complete breakdown of one's capacity to function professionally: clergy divorce, hospitalization, or rebellion and rejection by a family member of any activity that remotely resembles church. This category includes fractures or injuries that require constant attention by the clergy and/or congregation. For example, a pastor is perceived to be too much of a hugger, or the pastor and family are chronic spendthrifts. In another instance, the pastor may have suffered greatly from unrealized career expectations.

Inoperable or Incurable Injuries

The most serious wounds are a spiritual denial or rejection of the faith, gross moral turpitude, or deceptive and grossly manipulative behavior of a congregation against a pastor. This type of injury is not responsive to routine or constructive healing efforts and will undoubtedly result in termination of the relationship. Such endings themselves become, however painful, constructive acts of mercy, depending upon the reaction of the one wounded.

Obvious Injuries

This section will consider how day-by-day friction, abrasions, and wear and tear can be diagnosed, sorted out, and treated so as to minimize their negative impact on ministry. An obvious or superficial injury means more than silly or make-believe hurt. They are so self-evident that people often overlook the fact that symptoms point to deeper, more subtle injuries and conflicts. The injury analogy extends also to symptoms of theological stress and clergy-family conflicts that may occur in the form of daily financial headaches and heartaches. We have isolated four major causes of financial headaches and family heartaches.

Family Pressure to Lead and Interact. Ministry is a public activity and will always create pressure on family members, including spouse and children, to behave in a supportive or partnership role for the sake of the pastor. The pressure point is the expectation that the pastor and his/her family will always make positive contributions to leadership of the congregation. Surprisingly, in our survey the majority (sixty percent) of the pastors stated that the pressures associated with ministry were about as they expected. Ten percent reported that the pressures were not great enough to cause serious family problems. In families where the pastor and family members tend to be more introspective and do not have the personality or technical skills to engage in teaching, music leadership and performance, or to meet people openly and congenially, one can anticipate heartaches and headaches in the pastoral ministry.

The pastor may perceive that family members are shy and do not possess skills and talents typically desired by a congregation for full and active participation. Sometimes churches cherish unrealistic views of the pastor's family as spiritual mentors. The pastor must then intercede to defend and protect the family from stressful expectations that they participate in ways of which they are not capable. The pastor needs to set limits for his/her family's participation that are appropriate for the stage of marriage and family development. If the pastor refuses to give the family and the congregation guidance in this regard, heartaches and headaches for everyone will only increase. The pastor needs to learn to say a definite no to certain expectations and a joyous yes to other possibilities for service. In our judgment, it is reasonable to expect the pastor's family to engage in activities of their church.

Corresponding to the leadership qualities and skills is the frequently overlooked but nonetheless real fact of financial stress. Salaries may be less than the pastor requires to survive. Compounding the low basic salary stress is the expectation that out of that low salary the pastor will participate in a continual round of pizzas for the youth group, bowling, movies, miniature golf, and trips to recreational sites or theme parks as part of youth or adult outings. And the unwritten assumption is that as participants pastors should pay their own way. The frequent out-of-pocket expenses for the pastor and family add up quickly, yet they are expected and perhaps required to take part. So they should be reimbursed expenses. When these operating costs are coupled with a modest salary, the few dollars spent here and there quickly create financial headaches for the pastor. Often this is not recognized by the congregation.

As stated earlier, the majority of our respondents indicated that their salary package is either under $10,000 or falls into the $10,000–$15,000 range or the $20,000–$30,000 range. Nearly forty-four percent stated that it is not necessary for the spouse to work. While pastors typically cite low salary as a form of personal and family stress, many (forty-three percent) in our study consider their salary as average when compared to other pastors. However, when asked whether their own denomination pays adequately, fifty percent believe they are inadequately paid. This statistic is significant in that sixteen percent indicate uncertainty about this. That one-seventh of the pastors are uncertain suggests that a high percentage of respondents are trying to be nice by not saying that they are underpaid.

One way to relieve some of the financial headaches for the pastor is to make certain that more of the pastor's direct out-of-pocket expenses are reimbursed. Pastors frequently pick up the tab when out to lunch or coffee. While these incidental expenses may not seem like a lot, their cost over a year is considerable. Pastors need to learn to have enough grace either to go dutch treat or to allow others to pay.

A second problem is the fishbowl experience. The often-expressed complaint that the pastor's family lives in a fishbowl or glass house has some truth to it. However, our data suggest that clergy families are moving in nontraditional directions, such as separate careers of the clergy and clergy spouse. The expectation that the pastor's family will be the perfect exemplar of the Christian family is less prevalent. As more families within the congregation find it either financially necessary or personally desirable to have dual incomes, the stereotyping of the clergy family as a single-income family is disappearing. This is especially true in light of the dramatically increased percentage of women clergy in most denominations since 1970. The idea of the husband staying home to do the housework and rear the children on a full-time, non-income basis creates a welcome jarring of the traditional fishbowl.

A third area of symptomatic stress is the old complaint that the pastor is on call twenty-four hours a day. If time management principles are embraced, days off taken, and telephone-answering machines utilized, the pastor's anxiety in this matter will diminish. Pastors who claim that the need for privacy is the greatest disadvantage of being in the ministry should permit others to intercept people at the door, on the phone, or in the church office. Some are their own worst enemies. They almost invite invasion of privacy by encouraging people to call them any time of the day or night. And on the day off the pastor must not engage in church business.

The complaint of not enough time with family is the fourth major source of clergy stress and heartache. Often this lack of time with the family occurs because the pastor allows it. For example, one pastor was actively involved in supporting a parishioner who had been ordered by the county court to appear on abuse charges. The pastor had accompanied him to court twice, though the man's attorney failed to show up for the hearing because the parishioner had not bothered to do his homework. The pastor was convinced that the man had turned over a new leaf and wanted to translate his religious conversion into responsible behavior toward his wife and children, the pastor, and the court. But the date of the third court appearance was the very time of his children's closing program at their school. Ice cream and hot dogs would be served, and the pastor had promised his wife that he'd be present.

The pastor's dilemma: Should he be at court or at school? Because of our counsel the pastor went to the school program with his family. He advised the parishioner that he would not be in court, that the parishioner, his attorney, and the judge would have to work out things on their own. The results were amazing! The parishioner showed up on time with his attorney and the judge ruled for a suspended sentence. The pastor was not bogged down in a long morning in court. His kids were delighted and surprised that their dad showed up to have ice cream and hot dogs with them. They had a wonderful party and the kids showed off their father to their playmates and teachers. A flexible schedule allowed him to be with his kids at school when most parents were confined by a more restrictive work environment.

The pastor decided to trust God that the parishioner would be as responsible as he should be. In turn the pastor believed God would honor his decision, giving him peace about the decision and relaxation with his children. And it happened. But the pastor had to take the initiative to express trust in God, in a church member, and in himself that he did not have to be involved in everything and forego his long-planned hope to attend his kids' school program.

Spiritual Breakdowns. Obvious injuries are not limited to stress from finances or schedules or lack of privacy, but they include equally and perhaps more importantly the obvious breakdowns in spiritual strength that must be overcome. Our research indicates that there are four areas in which the obvious and most often neglected spiritual breakdowns occur.

Prayer and Meditation. On a daily basis the pastor needs time for prayer, meditation, and contemplation, These needs for spiritual preparation are not the same as the professional need to prepare for Bible studies, preaching, Sunday school discussions, or public presentations. The pastor clearly must maintain regular personal devotions for spiritual welfare. When the pastor neglects spiritual resources, healthful eating, or good work habits, the pastor panics when spiritual crises occur. An erosion of spiritual vitality sets in when the spiritual leader does not take care of her/his own relationship with God. When ministry is reduced to bare survival spiritually, the consequences include burnout and eventually disappointment and bitterness toward the church and its people.

Time Off. Pastors need time off. A rule of thumb states that a day off a week is better than saving up days for the ever-elusive and magic long weekend or extended vacation. Routine time off is essential for inner healing and itself is a form of spiritual retreat. Because pastors are busy on Sunday, that day is not a sabbath for the pastor. The biblical concept of sabbath is that of a time for reflecting on life's meaning and an opportunity for spiritual renewal.[1] Time off does not mean doing nothing. Instead, it means a change in activity and may include strenuous physical exercises, or it may be a day of inactivity to recharge physical, emotional, and spiritual batteries. The pastor's sabbath must be frequent enough and long enough to allow the body and the spirit to receive the grace of a personal sabbath. When a personal sabbath is not taken, the dangers are too apparent and are sadly expressed by a Lutheran pastor:

> I feel I have often neglected my family and didn't spend enough time with my children.

Bonding With the Kids. Not all ministers marry and have children. Some live in an empty nest. Jesus' words, "Let the little children come to me, and do not stop them; for it is to such as these that the kingdom of God belongs" (Luke 18:16, NRSV), is a call for the disciples and the pastor to receive the ministry of the simple, innocent, and transparent wisdom of children. Spiritual care of children is a vital part of one's ministry, and where a loving, nurturing relationship with children is avoided or neglected, whether in the pastor's family or with children in the church, we have a clear indication of spiritual breakdown.

Stress headaches occurred in one pastor's family in which the minister's wife was a schoolteacher. To forestall them the husband pastor, a warm and nurturing individual, assumed the responsibility in his daily routine to be at the house or stop by the house when the children arrived from school. This pastor took advantage of the two benefits of a career in the ministry that respondents to our survey value most highly: creative work and a flexible work schedule. His availability to his children and his help in mealtime preparation fostered bonding with the children, which is indeed rare. Such bonding is more than a family responsibility; it is a spiritual opportunity. True bonding goes beyond the earnest but impoverished commitment by one Presbyterian pastor who as a Christmas gift promised his young son thirty minutes a week of his undivided attention. The pastor as parent needs more genuine commitment. Thirty minutes a week may be a start, but it's hardly enough.

Family Vacation. Vacation time, like days off, calls for more than not doing anything. Vacation is a retreat and an opportunity for the pastor. As the toxic stress of spiritual and emotional exhaustion, which invariably builds up in the ministry, drains away, the pastor recoups spiritual, emotional, and physical resources and rebuilds relationships. The majority of our survey respondents (223 or forty percent) take a month off while 148 (twenty-six percent) take two weeks and 123 (twenty-two percent) have a three-week vacation, which is average for pastors. The vast majority (609 or eighty-one percent) indicate that they set aside a block of time for vacation. This is laudatory and should be part of any contractual agreement with a congregation. Vacation time itself may be a source of high stress, but it can be an opportunity for spiritual rebuilding and rebonding for the pastor and family members.

Deeper Injuries

Deeper injuries are more serious. They cannot be ignored or denied and will not respond to simple or minor changes in behavior. We've identified three areas of deeper injuries. They include "fractures in ministry," "chronic and annoyance problems," and "self-esteem injuries."

Fractures in Ministry. This image suggests serious breaks or breakdowns in ministry that cannot be easily or quickly resolved.

Failed Goals. Of the eight tasks of ministry mentioned in the previous chapter some may not have been accomplished, or perhaps the pastor is simply not capable of performing up to the standards and expectations of a church. It is not a matter of doing more, which does not solve the problem. The fracture is more serious than the church becoming more cooperative or understanding of a pastor's personal situation. Discussion about failed goals means that clearly recognized, stated, and defined expectations for goals are not achieved.

Like a marital breakup, pastor/congregation failures are not completely one party's fault. Failed goals create fractures, and the best way to correct such a fracture, simple or compound, is first to recognize its existence. The second step is to determine causes of the failure. And, third, either drop the goal or address it in a new way. To do otherwise would be like sending a patient to a physical therapist before going to an orthopedist who first must set the broken bone. Ignoring or misidentifying and therefore mistreating failed goals makes the pain difficult if not impossible to reach.

A Split in the Church. A split in the church can take other
forms than a significant portion of the membership leaving to
start a competitive congregation. The split may be a deep rift
over church goals, a proposed building program, a commitment
to start a day-care ministry or a shelter for the homeless or a
program of meals for the poor. Splits occur when a substantial
portion of the church refuses to cooperate and support a pastor
over stated programs, or if it openly attacks the efforts of the
pastor. Leadership must immediately assess the significance of
the split and determine to press and trust the Holy Spirit to heal.

Controversy Over Spiritual and Civil Issues. The pastor may
take a stand on abortion, civil rights, the flag, school prayer,
politics, etc. Or the failure of the church to live up to its own
spiritual mandate of witness, evangelism, and mission may
produce controversy. The pastor dare not adopt a cavalier
spiritual attitude of "damm the torpedoes, full speed ahead!" A
fracture over this type of controversy is a deep injury and cannot
be dismissed. The pastor is called to lead the congregation in
spiritual matters, and the congregation's reaction cannot be
treated lightly. The controversy must be aired within the life of
the church. This may require a congregational meeting with the
pulpit committee, board of deacons, vestry or session interven-
ing. Pastoral responsibilities are public spiritual mandates and
require public discussion and resolution.

Encounter with the Judicatory. A local congregation and its
pastor may be united in their understanding of ministry but at
sharp odds with pronouncements, official positions, or mandates
of denominational judicatory officials, whether at the regional or
national level. The response from denominational leaders may
be to talk about the importance of their all being one body in
Christ, which may mean that the local church needs to
straighten up and set aside its disagreements with the larger
church.

A number of pastors responding to the survey question,
"Attitude of denominational officials toward minister's family,"
reported that denominational officials were not supportive of
their ministry or family. In response to the request that pastors
categorize denominational officials as "understanding," "supportive," or "a source of problems," a high percentage felt
"uncertain": twenty-three percent about the "understanding"

category, twenty percent about the "supportive" category, and fifteen percent about the "source of problem" category.

When denominational officials are implicated in serious injuries to the pastor and family, the charges cannot be ignored, and a congregational committee must meet with the officials. Judicatory leaders are themselves representatives of the local church and the local church pastor. Therefore, they are accountable to the individual congregation and pastor as well as to denominational policy. When controversy arises, it may be wise for the pastor alone or in conjunction with a key lay leader or committee from the congregation to discuss with judicatory officials any injury to the body of Christ in the local church. These controversies are the same kind as those discussed in the Pastoral Epistles.

While claiming to be of one body with one Lord, denominational controversies still erupt. An Episcopal rector speaks of denominational leaders who maligned him:

> I was marginalized by the church hierarchy, and that caused many burdens and stresses.

Controversy and injury within the larger body cannot be ignored. Hierarchical conflicts cause serious damage and possible curtailment of the larger vision, mission, and ministry of the church. Judicatory officials represent supervisory and pastoral authority over a local church pastor, and if the pastor is not careful the conflict may become so inflamed that the pastor will fail to act with spiritual discernment and wisdom. Still, the final determination of who is "right" and who "wrong" must be attempted.

Chronic and Annoyance Problems. The fractures in ministry discussed above cannot be minimized, but less dramatic, painful, or obvious are injuries resulting from chronic difficulties. One of these could be the burden of an overwhelming debt a pastor may inherit from the former minister who inaugurated an ambitious but undersubscribed building program. This type of injury is not usually terminal, but a shifting of debt load does not eliminate the problem.

A second type of chronic problem is seen in the small minority of church members who sense an irresistible call to irritate the pastor. Regardless of the pastor's best efforts at a competent and conscientious ministry, criticisms swirl and rumors float. Most pastors are not and do not perceive themselves as being mean-spirited, and most find it difficult to accept the notion that not everyone is going to like them. Dissidents express displeasure in a number of demonstrable if not always vocal ways, and the pastor who is accustomed to believing that he or she is liked by everyone will invariably immerse family members and close friends in the irascibility of unhappy members. As a result, the pastor creates tension within the family or circle of friends because they can do little to stem the complaining and backbiting of spiritually immature church members. Every congregation will have an element of the disgruntled within it.

St. Paul himself was subjected to factions, rumors, and disappointments in his pastoral leadership. The contemporary pastor should not be surprised at the embodiment of the same type of restlessness and unhappiness with pastoral leadership. One of our respondents observed:

> At times there is criticism that is not easily taken. It does take an emotional toll that I am finally beginning to notice.

A third problem for the pastor is the family member who contemptuously expresses the belief that the congregation does not deserve the pastor's talent. Equally difficult is the overtly aggressive family member who tries to extract undue respect from the church. The pastor and her/his family may desire unwarranted financial improvement, increased vacation time, or greater recognition for professional competence. This kind of "help" from family members may not always be welcome by the pastor. While the pastor needs to protect the family from undeserved criticism and backbiting by unhappy church members, it is also the pastor's obligation to shield the congregation from unsolicited opinions from disgruntled family members. A Lutheran notes:

> My late wife would sometimes say, not always in jest, "I think you are married to the parish." I know some colleagues who get the same biting comments.

Perhaps a colleague or counselor can assist the family to place their reactions in a broader perspective and thereby reduce their level of frustration. Time alone does not heal this type of problem, but ignoring it does not relieve deeper injuries to ministry and self-esteem.

Self-Esteem Injuries. "Little things mean a lot" is the old saying. For each individual, self-esteem is a delicate, subtle, and fragile reality. Injuries to self-esteem often spring out of nowhere. We endeavor to protect our self-esteem by a number of devices. It may be denial. Or one may use gusto and exuberance to drive back the world, hoping thereby to prevent bringing the fragile ego to consciousness. One may mount a defensive counterattack against a trivial or senseless criticism because self-esteem, not a deed, is the felt target of a complaint. But counterattack is an ineffective strategy if one seeks long-term gains. The short-term benefit is a blocking of further damage to one's self-esteem. A dramatic example of this dynamic is offered by an Assemblies of God pastor:

> I have suffered a severe heart attack at age forty-seven, and my wife was hospitalized due to stress-related church problems.

Probably few if any laypeople there knew that the pastor regarded both his heart attack and his wife's hospitalization to be a direct result of stress provoked by the congregation.

A Church of God pastor shares a similar pain:

> After ten years at one church I resigned. Only later did I realize how stressed I was. Finally, following my doctor's advice I took a sabbatical.

Probable reasons for the resignation were personal, and perhaps the pastor could have cited other causes of the stress he was suffering. Some elements of his distress probably were not consciously part of his decision to resign.

A Lutheran pastor reported:

> When discontentment is expressed by members in the congregation, it is very difficult on the spouse. "Can't they see what they are doing to your enthusiasm?" my wife said to me more than once.

A second difficulty with injuries to the pastor's self-esteem is the minister's need to be loved. Ministers enjoy and are trained to use their nurturing gifts. Among highly nurturing people, self-esteem is often an exposed, sensitive aspect of life. A United Methodist pastor succinctly stated:

Tensions within the marriage as the result of ministry have caused my spouse to wonder how she can be an individual.

This pastor's wife apparently lived with so much pain and confusion that she was uncertain about her personal identity as a pastor's wife. When a congregation fails to appreciate a pastor and does not recognize the stress thus caused for family members, the pain is compounded.

Another Methodist pastor reflects a similar dilemma:

Many times my career became more important than my relationship with my husband—giving to others and not to him.

This pastor's need for congregational respect placed her in a conflict between wanting to love the congregation and realizing painfully late that she was not adequately loving her husband and family.

A pastor whose self-esteem is not strong is not able to build up the self-esteem of the congregation nor able to receive efforts from family members to build up the pastor's self-esteem.[2]

A third problem related to self-esteem is the feeling of being unappreciated. A United Methodist claimed:

Criticism in some situations causes us much stress, resulting in depression. There was a dislike for church even though the people themselves were not at fault.

Feeling caught in a self-esteem crossfire, this pastor reflects the dilemma and ease of projecting problems onto other people. He acknowledges that his congregation wasn't so much at fault as he first thought; nonetheless, the criticism and the pain jeopardize his self-esteem.

Another pastor speaks to the issue:

Criticism directed toward me affects all members of my family adversely. There is a tendency to be angry with each other.

A Presbyterian pastor rephrases the same problem:

We tend to be very "edgy" and critical of each other, always feeling hurried and in a rush.

Building self-esteem is probably one of the most important tasks in healing clergy-family injuries and conflicts. This can be helped along by setting limits on others' expectations of oneself, whether the congregation's, spouse's, children's, or one's own.

Self-inflicted criticisms indicate low self-esteem, which prevents the pastor from fully accepting the positive worth of what he/she is and has done. Susceptibility to self-esteem injuries underscores the need for prayer and meditation, time off for personal retreat and healing, the building of loving and bonding ties with family members, and the need for vacation time with family. In addition to dealing with emotional and physical stress, quiet, spiritual activities help build self-esteem.

Low self-esteem among the clergy is one of the deeper injuries in ministry, of which anorexia and bulimia are serious manifestations. Grandiose schemes and unrealistic goals are also efforts to compensate for it. Those not suffering from the problem have little idea of the extent of its crippling consequences, which are exceedingly difficult to correct because of its subtlety.[3] One develops higher levels of self-esteem by learning to recognize that one's life, ministry, emotions, feelings, and opinions really matter. Learning to say no to tasks may well be a way to say yes to the nurturing of self-esteem. That is, setting limits on ministerial tasks is the beginning of spiritual wisdom and self-esteem. It is a matter of appreciating one's self.

Incurable Injuries

Some conflicts and injuries are obvious and can be treated quickly. Results are directly observed. However, some incurable conflicts or breaks in faith directly affect one's personhood and ministry and are incurable and irreversible.

Family Breakup. We have identified three components to the family breakup that are irrevocable injuries.

A. Separation. Stress, incompatibility, and battle fatigue may result in stress levels so high that marital separation is inevitable. A Presbyterian pastor wrote:

> My wife had problems with [stress]. However, it was more a matter of her way of dealing with life in general and not of the ministry in particular.

This pastor's wife may have been naïve and weak, or the couple may have failed to recognize their incompatibility. The injury to ministry was so great that separation and divorce became inevitable.

Another pastor comments:

My first wife ran away. The children have managed to respect church while continuing to be involved.

A minister's stress gets under the skin of marriage partners to such an extent that the irritations become fatal to family relations. The lethal dosage of pastoral conflict may be a result of personality differences, the magnitude of pressures from work, or a clergy spouse unable to cope with stress rising from the triangle of pastor, church, and family.

A second force in marital separation is the social conflict in job and family role expectations. A United Methodist pastor comments:

My first husband expected both a traditional wife and mother and that I would fulfill my ministry in my spare time. We grew steadily apart.

Regardless of what the husband wanted from his clergy spouse, the incompatibilities were too great. Wife, mother, and ministry could not be contained within the limits of the marriage relationship.

Another cause is battle fatigue as poignantly expressed by a Methodist pastor:

My spouse has indicated that there is a real possibility she will not move with me at my next change of appointment.

And, lamentably, a young woman pastor reflects on the same dilemma:

My ministerial lifestyle has caused a broken engagement and cancellation of marriage plans.

Emotional fatigue or anticipated battle conflict strikes deep in the heart of a marriage, often creating irreversible problems.

B. Divorce. Commitments to ministry may be so intense that the pastor is willing to sacrifice a family member or a marriage for continued career stability. Our survey indicated that most spouses were aware that the marriage partner was entering the ministry. Incurable conflicts and injuries may be inflicted because a spouse does not know what he/she is getting into. Our data suggest that many ministers accept their spiritual call, but do not process the implications of that call for family members either at the beginning of the career, at midpoint, or after a number of years. A number of survey comments suggest that the greatest family stress and conflict came after many years of ministry. A Disciples pastor reported:

> In a previous church my wife and I had experienced a deep conflict in the congregation that affected us. I sought counseling. Then came the one-word conclusion, *divorce*.

Contributing to the problem is the clergy spouse's overwhelming sense of helplessness and powerlessness. A number of spouses indicated that the church had become the "mistress" of the pastor, draining away time, energy, and affection. We recommend that the spouse should be present whenever a pastor is involved in an interview in either a call or an appointment system. This practice will preclude the spouse's feeling like an unpaid staff member or even a partner in ministry. This can become the couples' safeguard against the congregation and the pastor's neglect or side-stepping of his/her obligation to spouse and family. Comments on the survey indicate that family members perceive themselves to be alienated and neglected in these significant interview occasions where promises and expectations are set in concrete in the minds of the clergy and committee but that are not communicated to the pastor's family. Often wrong conclusions are drawn and improper suggestions offered that the pastor's family is but a happy, obedient extension of the pastor's ego.

C. Uncontrollable Children. Not all family breakups are constituted by a separation or marital divorce. The breakup or alienation of parents and children is also frequently seen. A United Methodist pastor reports:

> A teenage son rebelled and hasn't rejoined the family. Abusive people caused some thought of my leaving the ministry. Our family was stifled by parish circumstances.

A Nazarene pastor describes the irreversible pressures on his children:

> Our children have changed churches because they thought we were unfairly treated.

A Presbyterian pastor offers:

We have experienced marital difficulties, and our older child has had significant problems with drugs and alcohol, self-identity, and decision making. We feel much stress in our family.

A UCC pastor comments:

One child has left the church and denies faith in Christ.

This complaint was seconded by another UCC pastor:

I'm not sure I can blame it on the ministry but one child has faltered.

Some of the rebellion of children may be only a developmental stage for the children. The examples cited by the Nazarene and UCC pastors, however, indicate hard-core spiritual rebellion. The stress may somehow be managed by the pastor and spouse but not handled well by the children. The likelihood of their returning to the denomination or even to the Christian faith is, from a human perspective, unlikely. Nothing can be done apart from relying on the grace of God to bring the wayward lamb back to the fold. The children, if we are to believe the pastor's comments, were driven out by excessive stress in the ministry.

In many cases pastors' low self-esteem and compulsion to keep everything looking good, under control, happy, content, and sailing smoothly (for the sake of appearance) create tremendous stresses on the children. Children are incredibly perceptive; they quickly sense that something is wrong: tension, conflict, arguments, and fights followed by long periods of stony silence, blaming, or avoidance behavior. They may believe that they are the source of the problem inasmuch as their parents won't tell them anything. Parents may fail to understand that emotional, financial, or career-related problems should be openly discussed with children who are over six years of age.

If children are to develop a strong sense of self-esteem, pastor and spouse must confide in them so that all the family can grow through the problems. But parents experiencing marital difficulties do not want to be subjected to children's intense scrutiny. A child may charge the parent with stupidity, naïveté, or insanity for accepting killer work hours, taking no time off, or spending very little time with the family; but the pastor doesn't want to be told the truth by her/his own children. When communication fails, children have little recourse except to build up resentment, bitterness, and distrust. When old enough to rebel, they may use drugs, alcohol, non-Christian religions, the occult, or atheism to make a protest statement.

Serious family problems may involve separation, threat of divorce, or hard-core rebellion by children. It is essential for the pastor to advise the church committee responsible for his/her care and oversight. It is tough on self-esteem for the pastor to admit that problems exist. Frequently, many members of the congregation will offer a helpful, sympathetic response, if the pastor will admit to a need. That is how we bear one another's burdens.

The children will understand that an admission of need like this is not easy on the clergy parent, but a request for help or reduction in workload or whatever on the part of the pastor/parent is a step in the right direction. When children know that dad or mom is going to bat for them, they will be more responsive and accommodating. When injuries of the magnitude just described occur, the pastor is under a spiritual, emotional, and professional mandate to reach out for help and to give help to family members.

Church Breakup. Sometimes conflicts within a congregation are so severe that the congregation breaks up, or it may break off from the denominational or parent organization. The cause may be a theological controversy, irreconcilable differences over a social issue, or simply a power move within the congregation between two warring factions. Usually these forces are politically, personally, and spiritually beyond the ability of the pastor to reverse. These cleavages are the organizational principalities and powers of this world at work.

Many pastors jump to take responsibility for matters that far exceed their call as agents of Christ to the world. Pastors may accept too much blame for congregational breakup, but deep conflicts within the congregation often have very little to do with a pastor's personality or leadership style. As in marriage breakups, stories behind those in the church also have two sides. When the dispute erupts because of denominational rather than local church activity or pronouncements on controversial issues, the pastor cannot be held at all responsible. He or she may side with either party and may decide to resign and regroup with a remnant to rebuild the ministry. While pastors

tend to regard themselves as spiritual watchdogs whose responsibility it is to keep the family or church intact, a corrective step
in relinquishing the overly conscientious and responsible
leadership styles would be helpful for pastors.[4]

Issues of codependency, even to personality characteristics of
"adult children of alcoholics" (ACOA) certainly apply to many
pastors. This clinical analogy suggests that clergy assume too
much responsibility or become irresponsible in their frustrated
perfectionism. Compulsion to make certain that the kingdom
and the church always come out looking good is a dangerous
spiritual and psychological drive. Pastors are too protective of a
congregation or the denomination. Like an abused child or a
child of an alcoholic they overprotect and overinvolve themselves in a conspiracy of silence, working always with a smile
that masks pain, abuse, fear, and dread. Always under control or
radically out of control, pastors need to learn to smile less and
cry more, to release more, and be more vulnerable. This will
help reduce the fear of the "church abuse" and "parishioner
rejection" that is seen so frequently in abusive and alcoholic
families and is so prevalent among service-oriented careers.[5]

Midcareer Exits. The call to Christian ministry is a lifelong
commitment to ministry. Clergy and laity alike are called into
ministry. The ordained clergy are set apart not for privilege or
status but for servanthood and as formal representatives of the
denomination. Some ordained pastors do not realize the implications of a call. Others are like Jonah whom God called to a
ministry in Nineveh. He did not want to give up the security and
stability of his Jerusalem quintessential pastorate, a political
plum in the capital of Jewish piety.

Some people fight the call within the call, and their ministries
become spiritually shallow, socially conflicted, and riddled with
controversy of one form or another. Whether one's call shifts to
lay status, whether family problems are insurmountable or there
is a continual avoidance of the full claim of the Gospel,
midcareer exits occur for a minority of pastors. Exits should be
considered by other pastors whose spiritual zeal, enthusiasm,
and dedication to ministry and church have long since vanished.
In our findings, we see a pattern of four types or reasons for
midcareer exit.

The first one is a response to unbelievable conflicts within the parish. These may manifest themselves as poor health, stress, or conflicts in the area of spiritual values. An American Baptist pastor concedes:

[We are experiencing] depression, loneliness, thoughts of leaving the ministry, and hostility toward members who are nonsupportive.

This pastor caught in the throes of deep alienation and the seeming impossibility of coping with the stress has seriously considered leaving the ministry.

A Disciples pastor reports:

Pressure to leave [the pastorate] resulted in extensive depression.

Pastors who leave their ministry for other career choices, whether voluntarily or under duress, report an overwhelming sense of defeat, depression, guilt, family dislocation, remorse, and inability to cope quickly and adjust readily to new work situations. A Lutheran pastor says succinctly:

The stress may result in health problems.

That is a brief word, but it is an echo of many clergy about stress that translates into personal health problems and family illnesses. Some are severe enough to break up the family or to require extensive counseling; or the decision is to get out from under the load of ministry altogether.

A second major source of midcareer exit is family needs. A Methodist pastor reports:

[The stress on my family and me] led to a near breakdown before I learned to adjust.

Family needs cannot be overlooked. Another Methodist pastor reports:

I am unable to find a place to serve where my husband's job is, or he is unable to find suitable work where a church is in which I could minister.

Another pastor who chose not to leave says of the consequent divorce:

Obviously my divorce was stressful. Time commitments and choices to do the work of the church rather than be with family are still stressful.

Another way of solving the problem without exiting is stated by a Nazarene pastor:

[Stress is less] severe since Sally has eagerly joined in the ministry and feels called to minister.

This pastor recruited his wife into the partnership form of ministry as a way of relieving stress and avoiding "the exit." Had Sally not been cooperative, the pastor's response suggests that ministry would have been curtailed, if not ended.

A PCA pastor reflects upon the tension in his calling:

[I've had] problems in doubting my call to the ministry.

From a more physical aspect a PCUSA pastor comments:

[Stress from] minor worries or discouragement or frustration has aggravated chronic problems/diabetes, high blood pressure, and cholesterol.

Finally, another pastor reported:

Your [survey] form arrived the day I was being put on disability for "burnout."

The need to keep the family healthy and one's body and spirit alive may force pastors to leave the ministry either for a short period to regroup and heal or to leave permanently. We support the idea of churches encouraging midcareer entrance into ministry, but we also support the fact that midcareer exits ought to be made easier. If reasons for leaving are valid, then responsible officials in the congregation and denomination should go the second mile to reassure the pastor that adequate exit counseling and new-career guidance are provided. Conversely, pastors dare not wait until incurable spiritual, emotional, or physical injuries rise before asking for help.

A third area of stress that leads to midcareer exits is ministerial peer relationships. Clergy peer-group support is offered in both formal and informal settings for those whose behavior and attitudes are acceptable. But the pastor who dares to be a prophet, whose personality may be abrasive or out of sync with the dominant peer ethos within the denomination or within the community where the pastor ministers may experience extreme peer pressure not to stay in the ministry. If the pastor is guilty of a sin that calls for his/her dismissal, the exit may result from formal legal action, may be settled out of court, or resolved through plea bargaining.

The informal judge and jury of ministerial peers may be less forgiving than a formal judgment. Fellow pastors may be angry with or intolerant of a local congregation or a church judicial system that dares to forgive a pastor. Such conflicts resulting from peer professional pressures are relentless and may result in ostracism of the pastor, an action that will leave the pastor no choice but to make a midcareer exit.

A pastor's new interests are a fourth reason for an exit. The need to meet any number of family responsibilities may shift the pastor's more focused interest in new directions. It takes a lot of courage for a pastor whose interests have shifted actually to leave the ministry.

Earlier we argued that one should not plunge impulsively into ministry without prayer, meditation, and extended conversations with spiritual superiors. By the same token, leaving the ministry should not be done unadvisedly or impulsively without prayer, consultation with older members of the church, and deep and thoughtful conversations with the family members most directly affected.

Because of health and financial pressures, we anticipate more midcareer exiting in mainline denominations as a result of the increase in dual-career marriages. In our survey, the smaller and more conservative denominations have fewer clergy who leave or anticipate leaving for strictly family and economic needs. Although these pastors may have reasons for leaving that are as valid as those of others, they tend to feel that a call to ministry is a permanent one "for better or for worse."

Coping With Bumps and Bruises in Ministry

Inevitable Bumps and Bruises in Ministry

We have identified eight aspects of ministry that seem to create the day-in, day-out bumps and bruises for pastors. Like physical bumps and bruises, spiritual ailments don't have to be catastrophic crises, but if left unattended, abused, or treated improperly, they can lead to serious, debilitating, and conceivably permanent and life-threatening injury.

Finances. While most reporting pastors felt that their pay was commensurate with the size of church and their type of ministry, financial stress is a recurring theme in the comments offered in our surveys. The problems with finances are twofold. The one concerns lack of sufficient income to sustain the pastor and his/her family on a day-by-day basis. There is an inverse correlation between the calling and the belief that one is paid enough. The clearer the call, the fewer the complaints; and income is less frequently the measure of ministry. For those pastors whose sense of vocation is not so sharp, finances become a measure of personal worth and affect self-esteem.

A second problem area in clergy finances relates to the expense of serving the clergy family's debt. Pastors need to move more toward the biblical injunction to live free of debt. This is a counterculture suggestion to those retailers who encourage buyers to charge everything and worry about payment later. Our recommendation would be that as far as possible the pastor set as a goal a debt-free life. The United Methodist *Discipline* asks this question of each candidate for ordination, "Are you in debt so as to embarrass you in your work?" Years ago Methodist episcopal leaders and pastors chuckled at John Wesley's question. Today fewer and fewer snickers are heard. Pastors are known to file for bankruptcy or leave scandalous debts when they move from a community. Larry Burkett is an advocate of debt-free living, and he admonishes pastors about Christian conscientiousness and a high level of fiscal integrity in ministry.[6]

Heavy Workload. Many pastors complain about the number of work hours per day, the long evening sessions they are required to attend, and the fact that church work goes on seven days a week. While many pastors complain about the work pressure, one pastor declares himself a martyr:

I tend to be a workaholic.

There is a difference, though, between the true workaholic and the one who works increasing numbers of hours and at the same time grows more dissatisfied with work. Many ministers waste time tallying the long hours, yet time spent in actual productive work is very little. But they enjoy complaining.

The solution to the heavy workload is suggested by the

responses to our survey and in a humanitarian concern for the pastor and family. One United Methodist pastor reports:

> My spouse is concerned about members' criticism, whether or not criticism is deserved. [My] time is another factor; everybody wants [some of] it. I feel a need to give all I can.

From the aspect of physical strength, most pastors give more time than they should. As we have said before, they need to negotiate for days off each week, at least two weeks vacation, and opportunity for continuing education and study. They should not involve themselves in church-related meetings five nights a week, and they need to reserve one or two nights a week for family life.

Pastors simply must go beyond the commitment of the one quoted earlier who thought he was doing something significant in giving minutes a week to his son. If a pastor has given very little time, thirty minutes is a quantum leap forward. It is, however, a minuscule step toward a serious commitment to family.

Pressure on Family. One pastor reported:

> The kids were severely affected by the congregation's criticism of me. Rejection of me and of them left them isolated. The result of their [consequent] low self-esteem only now is subsiding.

Criticism and pressures will come, and the pastor must realize that not only is his or her own life under scrutiny but also those of a spouse and, more vitally, of one's children. Everything from criticism of the congregation to the changing of school systems, the loss of friends, the alienation of children from church are indications of pressures on the family. At some point most pastors will have to make a decision about whether to pursue selfish career advancement or, out of Christian love and dedication to the family make career sacrifices on their behalf. If the family understands that loving sacrifices are being made because of them, we expect that both spouse and children will be more responsive to and appreciative of the pastor. Nurture of the family must be accomplished in small increments and on a day-to-day basis. Waiting to take time for the family during the big blast weekend or the magnificent vacation won't do because those occasions have ways of never materializing because of unexpected crises within the parish family or within the pastor's own family.

Physical Deterioration of the Pastor or Family Members. A Nazarene pastor cites his sources of stress:

Physical problems, emotional problems, and doubting my call to the ministry at times.

A PCA pastor notes:

Two years ago I asked my officers to provide for my disability coverage. It was treated poorly although the church is financially sound. Now it is hard to love them.

A PCUSA pastor comments:

I've been in counseling learning to deal with anger, stress, and feelings of inadequacy.

Mental and emotional health are at the forefront of pastors' concern. They commented about spouses receiving counseling for depression, about high blood pressure, about children getting involved in alcohol or drugs, and about other problems like alienation. One UCC pastor comments:

In the move to the current pastoral setting our son made a suicide attempt: there was great difficulty in separation from the last parish for him.

Physical ailments are basically a way that the body tells the individual of acute inner trauma. Pastors report this trauma as stress, pressure, etc. Physical manifestations are less a result of poor health than evidence of high stress levels. Back to basics: The pastor needs to take a day off, be guaranteed of a night or two at home per week, time for family outings, or evenings with friends. A solid block of time earmarked for vacation and planned by the whole family will do wonders to relieve both emotional stress and physical ailments. The pastor must realize that there are limits to the number of responsibilities that one can handle well. Such restraints cut down on complaints and a pastor's reaching out to the family for support needed due to overextension.

Disregard of Children. Pastors who responded to our survey showed a sensitivity to their children but also an acute sense of guilt about the effects upon their children of the workload, stress, and bickering with family members. The most frequently voiced complaint was over children who had become so alienated from the church that either they sought another faith group, were totally alienated from and turned off by the church altogether, or had "spiritually flipped out" to become part of a denomination at the opposite end of the theological spectrum of their parent's church and ministry.

Spending special time with the children is essential if they are to know that they are important to the minister. Unique times of going for walks, taking the children individually or collectively for ice cream and special treats are low cost but important gestures. For most people it is not the cost in terms of going to fancy restaurants, movies, or elaborate trips. Most people, and especially children, are satisfied simply by spending undivided, undistracted time with parents.

Another rationale for telephone-answering machines is to guarantee that time spent with children will not be interrupted. Constant interruptions communicate to children that their time and lives are not important. Otherwise, the parent gives the impression that any interruption is more important than the relationship with the child. The rhetorical question for the pastor is whether one would interrupt a conversation with a denominational official or the President of the United States to answer the phone. Apart from the spouse, one's children are the most highly valued relationship for the pastor.

Emphasis on Church Growth. Most of the literature on church growth is oriented toward numbers and statistics and the mobility of adults rather than ministry in areas of genuine need. A theological fallacy shared by many pastors and denominational officials is that if one has a larger church membership, more money will be available and a more adequate budget can be raised. If the emphasis is placed on actual ministry to real needs of people, the budget will not be a problem. Spiritually, "where there is a will there is a way." Pastors must move beyond the obsession with statistics and homogeneous church membership and growth. We suggest that if there is genuine ministry to meet real needs, the budget will be met and the preoccupation with church growth will disappear and take care of itself.

Absorption in Promotion. Unlike most professions the incremental financial change from one pastorate to another is small, and pastors become obsessed with what they might need to do to get a church that is a little larger and a salary that is (usually insignificantly) larger. Salaries are important, but a sure sign of a pastor who is in trouble is one who romanticizes and fantasizes about how the next church will be a pastoral mecca where everything works out. It won't.

Ministry is where you are now, not where you think you'd like to be. The age-old dilemma of the disciples arguing about who was going to be first in the kingdom of God extends into the backrooms of ministry today. The language may be sanitized, but spiritual greed and insecurity are still evident. To be preoccupied with promotion is to be obsessed by those concerns that become deep-seated bruises on the body of Christ. Each part of the body has its own function, integrity, and contribution to the overall ministry. Through prayer, meditation, and rededication, pastors need to wait for Jesus to tell them to put their nets down on the other side of their present ministry. Too many flail at their current situations and fail of their opportunities because they are unwilling to hear the call and catch the vision of their present congregations. That call and not the hoped-for call to a promotion should be a matter of utmost spiritual concern for the pastor.

The Congregational Antagonist. Every congregation has its critics. They may or may not be the same ones who plagued the predecessor. But critics they are and they will always be. A pastor dare not react negatively to every breath of criticism and controversy that comes. A second problem is the roadblock that the antagonist is to the higher calling of ministry. A third problem is that the pastor must deal with critics and antagonists with integrity. If not, the pastor carries the negativity and passive aggressiveness home. The pastor is seen by family as wishy-washy, uncertain, and confused about his/her pastoral identity, and family members will not take a stand with either the congregation or the pastor. That negative witness is permission, whether or not consciously understood, for a spouse or child to become disenchanted, disrespectful, and unsupportive of the pastor in his/her congregational ministry.

Stepping Back and Going Again. As the bumps and bruises, aches and pains of ministry in the eight areas inflict themselves upon the pastor, the temptation to fight or flee can be overcome by deliberate, prayerful stepping back, reassessing the situation, and beginning anew. The pastor does not have the resources to do this unless there is a day off a week, time with the family in the evening, vacation time, and opportunity for intellectual and cultural growth through continuing study and personal development. An American Baptist pastor complained:

> [I was] unable to pursue interests (cultural and academic). It was difficult to establish friends. The isolation and the integration of personal into ministerial experience did not occur.

By developing outside interests that renew and stimulate, the pastor engages in a sabbath experience and is thereby enabled to reflect on the meaning of both pastoral ministry and life in general. Some pastors do this through a leave of absence, others through counseling, and others find family psychotherapy a valuable way of regrouping. Some meet with spiritual guides. Others are able to draw on family resources that are mutually supportive to process the conflict. The pastor must have the capacity to disengage from the everyday work level and load so as to regroup with the family. This need not necessarily be an escape or evasion. Our challenge is the continuing need to receive a sabbath on a daily basis so ministry and life are seen from a proper perspective.

Stepping-Stones to Growth. In developing the capacity to step back, reevaluate, and regroup, one begins to utilize what we call the eight stepping-stones to growth. In the survey we identified the eight highest ranking significant advantages that pastors report about ministry.

The first is creative work. Overall, pastors want to engage Christ, the community, the church, themselves and their families in creative work, and they see the church as a wonderful opportunity to live out the challenges of Christian ministry. Constructive, creative opportunities of Christian ministry should never be stifled. Where the pastor loses the creative or cutting edge, the first stepping-stone has become dislodged.

The second opportunity is the flexible schedule. Nevertheless, the complaints registered in our study indicate that pastors do not use that advantage wisely and end up with insufferable and inflexible schedules. If flexibility is important—and it is—then the pastor needs to retain that flexibility of schedule both to complement creativity and to increase performance. The advantage of a flexible schedule is that the pastor can be creative at those times in the day or the week that are most constructive.

The third stepping-stone is the opportunity for study. It is not enough to gain an education, to be ordained, to start a family and to live happily ever after. Maintaining one's intellectual and emotional growth is best symbolized by the stepping-stone of opportunities for continuing education, retreats, study, and intellectual enlightenment. This is especially true for pastors who have to spend so much of their time teaching, preaching, leading, and guiding. For a number of years some denominations have required that pastors take a certain amount of continuing education each year.

While the first three-stepping stones to growth involve the pastor's personal life, the fourth one, support from the congregation, is a declaration that the most important support group for the pastor is not peer professionals nor denominational officials but the active, lively support of the congregation. Many comments on the survey made clear the fact that congregational support was inadequate, lacking, or negative. But in the process of responding to the inevitable pressures by stepping back and regrouping, many pastors discovered that the congregation was prepared to be far more supportive of and sensitive to the pastor and the pastor's family than the pastor had imagined earlier in the ministerial career. We are one body in Christ and the basic support of the congregation for the pastor personally, for the pastor's family, and for the call to ministry is essential in coping with the everyday stresses of pastoral responsibility.

The fifth significant way of dealing with the stresses of everyday life is the claim on the surveys that the spouse is able to participate both in the church and in the ministry of the pastor. Only infrequently can a husband and wife work together in their career development. When society was primarily an agrarian or "mom and pop" entrepreneurial business, one saw numerous examples of families working together. This situation is seen far less often now except on the farm or where spouses have the same career training. Society has become far more technical and jobs so highly differentiated that in many families husband and wife can scarcely understand the shop talk or technical language of each other's career. It is important for the pastor that the spouse, in some measure, participate in the congregational ministry. It is clear that not all spouses want to be involved at a high level so as to be perceived as a partner. Nor do all pastors desire it. At the same time, it is *essential* for the minister that the spouse be supportive of ministry and participate at some level that seems appropriate to the spouse and that is in keeping with his/her spiritual and leadership talents. It is wise to encourage the spouse to participate in the ongoing life of the church and to share in decision making and debriefing of daily pastoral activities.

The sixth most important measure of coping with daily difficulties is the ready-made friends offered to the pastor by the body of Christ, the local congregation. By this phrase, we mean that there is a shared worldview, belief system, activities, value system, and standards of moral behavior that build in an immediate support group of friends in the congregation. The culture in general is so diffused, pluralistic, and heterogeneous that one may work for years with a colleague and scarcely get to know what that individual really believes or thinks or does when away from work. By contrast the church provides a ready-made community of friends that should not be quickly dismissed. Our footnote to this stepping-stone is the conviction that the pastor's friendship base and membership group should extend outside the life of the church. Outside relationships, in the first place, are a place of ministry for the pastor; another reason to cultivate friends from beyond the congregation simply is the personal enrichment one receives from exchanging ideas with those who do not have the same worldview and subscribe to the same value system as the pastor and the congregation.

The seventh important aspect of coping with daily problems is job security. In a time when forty-year-old white collar managers are being fired en masse from American industries (or so it almost seems), the benefit of job security is more significant. The value of job security ran across the eleven denominations and was not limited to those denominations, such as the United Methodist Church, where the appointive process tends to ensure greater job security. Job security was certainly not the most important factor because ministry is a spiritual vocation, and an issue such as security tends to run counter to creative work and flexible schedules.

Many pastors are naïve about the stresses and demands placed on even skilled and highly qualified professionals, including those with earned doctorates in speciality areas. Jobs are hard to come by and retain without disruption or layoffs for long periods of time. The change in growth and technical knowledge is so rapid that few people are going to retire at the job they began with. For pastors that is not the case, and, while the financial grass may look greener on the other side of the career fence, job stability certainly is not numbered among those things one can count on in careers outside the ministry.

The final stepping-stone or way of coping with everyday struggles for the pastor is support from other clergy. It is not surprising that support for clergy from fellow clergy is important, but it is secondary to the importance to clergy (as we've said over and over) of creative work and schedule flexibility. We consider that good. Otherwise, one runs the risk of forming a clergy union that gains a vested interest in keeping clergy employed regardless. Support, love, affection, constructive criticism, and honest feedback from other clergy are important. The pastor who is a loner in today's pastoral world will not go far without stumbling or receiving unnecessary bumps and bruises. The active and creative camaraderie with fellow clergy is essential for the pastor's ongoing effectiveness.

Increased Diagnostic Skills. Our goal in this chapter, as in the entire study, is to help pastors learn to understand better their own calling, and to engage helpfully in accurate diagnosis of injuries, conflicts, and problems. Are they superficial, deeper and serious injuries, or in fact incurable conflicts? To distinguish a serious problem from ordinary wear and tear of everyday activity is important. This chapter is dedicated to helping pastors develop a more self-critical evaluation and discover the origins of stress, conflicts, illnesses, rebellion, and family disruptions. As pastors learn to evaluate more adequately the dynamics of their own situation, their vocation, and how their vocation is likely to thrust pressures upon themselves and families, the more effective will be their ministry both to and with their families and their congregations.

In a positive way, one's spiritual self-confidence in theological and vocational diagnosis will best be expressed in a heartfelt acceptance of the statement in chapter five: "The burden of proof rests upon me as pastor to make the the best of my calling because I believe that God has called me to an active, sacrificial, and fulfilling ministry."

Notes

Chapter 1

[1]Raymond J. Lawrence, Jr., *The Poisoning of Eros: Sexual Values in Conflict* (New York: Augustine Moore, 1989), 38.1.

[2]Ibid., 39.

[3]F. F. Bruce, *Paul: Apostle of the Heart Set Free* (Grand Rapids: Eerdmans, 1977), 269.

[4]Lawrence, op. cit., 56.

[5]Ibid., 64–65.

[6]G. Martellet, "Sixteen Christological Theses on the Sacrament of Marriage," in *Contemporary Perspectives on Christian Marriage*, ed. Richard Malone and John R. Connery (Chicago: Loyola University Press, 1984), 275.

[7]Ibid., 278.

[8]See Cameron Lee and Jack Balswick, *Life in a Glass House*, Chapter 2, "Triangles in the Pastoral Ministry" (Grand Rapids: Zondervan, 1989), 29–56.

[9]Wilhelm Ernst, "Marriage As Institution and the Contemporary Challenge to It," in *Contemporary Perspectives on Christian Marriage*, op. cit., 63–69.

[10]Margaret H. Watt, *The History of the Parson's Wife* (London: Faber and Faber, 1945), 12.

[11]Ibid.

[12]Wallace Denton, *The Role of the Minister's Wife* (Philadelphia: Westminster, 1962), 22.

[13]Ibid., 25.

[14]Watt, op. cit., 69.

[15]Ann Douglas, *The Feminization of American Culture* (New York: Knopf, 1977), 91. Also see E. Brooks Holifield, *A History of Pastoral Care in America: From Salvation to Self-Realization* (Nashville: Abingdon, 1983).

[16]Welthy Honfinger Fisher, *Handbook for Ministers' Wives* (New York: Woman's Press, 1950), 71.

[17]Carolyn P. Blackwood, *The Pastor's Wife* (Philadelphia: Westminster, 1951), 13.

[18]Maxine Haines, *The Ministry We Share: A Manual for the Wesleyan Pastor's Wife* (Marion, Ind.: Wesley Press, 1986).

Chapter 2

[1]Frances Trott, *Our Call* (Wayne, N.J.: Sheba Press, 1973). See p. 10 for Abigail Wootton Painter's musings.

[2]John Calvin, *Institutes of the Christian Religion*, ed. John T. McNeill; trans. and indexed by Ford Lewis Battles (Philadelphia: Westminster, 1960), IV:iii.10.

[3]Glen E. Whitlock, *From Call to Service: The Making of A Minister* (Philadelphia: Westminster, 1946), 22.

Chapter 3

[1]Daniel Levinson, *The Exceptional Executive: A Psychological Conception* (London: Oxford University Press, 1968), 260–61, 264–65.

[2]Anonymous. MMPI test profiles for ministers were made available from ministers not included in the study.

[3]Robert C. Carson, "Appendix A, Interpretive Manual to the MMPI" in *MMPI Research Developments and Clinical Applications* (New York: McGraw-Hill, 1969), 289.

[4]Cameron Lee and Jack Balswick, *Life in a Glass House* (Grand Rapids: Zondervan, 1989), chapter 9.

[5]William G. T. Douglas, *Ministers' Wives* (New York: Harper & Row, 1965).

[6]Bill Everett, "The Faith of Couple Careers: Exploring Alternate Vocational Patterns" (Paper presented to the Society for the Scientific Study of Religion, October 29, 1989).

Chapter 4

[1]See Dianne K. Kieren and Brenda Munro, "Handling Greedy Clergy Roles: Dual Clergy Example," *Pastoral Psychology* 36 (Summer 1988): 239–48.

Chapter 5

[1]Dennis M. Campbell, *The Yoke of Obedience* (Nashville: Abingdon, 1988), 106.

[2]Personal correspondence from Thomas A. Robinson, April 21, 1990. In addition to his ministerial credentials (M.Div., Duke University, 1989), he holds a J.D. degree from Wake Forest University, 1973.

[3]John Boley is an attorney (J.D. degree, Case Western Reserve, 1983) and student at Duke Divinity School (M.Div., 1992).

Chapter 6

[1]Elizabeth O'Connor, *Letters to Scattered Pilgrims* (New York: Harper & Row, 1979), 1–5.

[2]Leroy Howe, "Between the Generations: Healing the Hurts and Reconciling the Differences," *Perkins Journal* 1 (January/April 1990): 6.

[3]See Hazelden's study book, *Keep Coming Back* (San Francisco: Harper & Row/Hazelden Foundation, 1988); Melody Beattie, *Beyond Codependency and Getting Better All the Time* (San Francisco: Harper & Row/Hazelden Foundation, 1989); Stephanie Covington and Liana Beckett, *Leaving the Enchanted Forest* (San Francisco: Harper & Row, 1988).

[4]Lou Louder, "Theological Perspectives on Alcoholic Family Systems," (Th.M. thesis, The Divinity School of Duke University, 1984), 55. The thirteen steps from *Adult Children of Alcoholics* by Janet Geringer Woititz, (Florida: Health Communications, 1983), 55–94:

1. Adult children of alcoholics guess at what normal is.
2. Adult children of alcoholics have trouble following a project through from beginning to end.
3. Adult children of alcoholics lie when it would be just as easy to tell the truth.
4. Adult children of alcoholics judge themselves without mercy.
5. Adult children of alcoholics have difficulty having fun.
6. Adult children of alcoholics take themselves very seriously.
7. Adult children of alcoholics have difficulty with intimate relationships.
8. Adult children of alcoholics overreact to changes over which they have no control.
9. Adult children of alcoholics constantly seek approval and affirmation.
10. Adult children of alcoholics usually feel different from other people.
11. Adult children of alcoholics are super-responsible or super-irresponsible.
12. Adult children of alcoholics are extremely loyal, even in face of evidence that the loyalty is undeserved.
13. Adult children of alcoholics tend to lock themselves into a course of action without giving serious consideration to alternative behaviors or possible consequences. This impulsivity leads to confusion, self-loathing, and loss of control of their environment. As a result, they spend tremendous amounts of time cleaning up the mess.

[5]Ann Wilson Schaef, *Co-Dependence: Misunderstood–Mistreated* (San Francisco: Harper & Row, 1986).

[6]Larry Burkett, *Debt-Free Living* (Chicago: Moody, 1989), 72–73. Also see, William W. Wells, *The Agony of Affluence* (Grand Rapids: Zondervan, 1989.)

Appendix

Survey of the Clergy Family

This is the survey instrument sent to ministers. The data and extrapolation of the data in this book are based upon survey results.

1. Sex: _____ Male _____ Female

2. Race   ☐ White
            ☐ Black
            ☐ Other (state) _____

3. Highest level of   ☐ high school   ☐ some seminary
   education
                      ☐ Bible school   ☐ seminary graduate
                      ☐ some college   ☐ graduate work be-
                                                  yond seminary
                      ☐ college graduate
   List degrees/diplomas received _____

4. Years in the ministry. Begin with the year you were fully ordained or became pastor or associate pastor of a church.
   ☐ under 5   ☐ 15–19
   ☐ 5–9   ☐ 20–29
   ☐ 10–14   ☐ 30 and over

5. How old were you when you were first appointed to or called by a local church?
   ☐ under 25   ☐ 30–34   ☐ 40–44   ☐ 50 and over
   ☐ 25–29   ☐ 35–39   ☐ 45–49

6. How many different congregations or charges have you served as pastor or associate pastor?
   ☐ 1   ☐ 4   ☐ 7   ☐ 10 or more
   ☐ 2   ☐ 5   ☐ 8
   ☐ 3   ☐ 6   ☐ 9

7. What is the average Sunday morning worship attendance of the church(es) you are now serving?
   ☐ under 25   ☐ 100–149   ☐ 350–499

☐ 25–49   ☐ 150–199   ☐ 500–999
☐ 50–99   ☐ 200–349   ☐ 1000 and over

8. What is your present position   ☐ Pastor
in the church?   ☐ Associate Pastor
    ☐ Other (state) _____

9. In what size community is your current church located?
☐ rural open country   ☐ small city 2,500–10,000
☐ village under 250   ☐ medium sized city 10,000
☐ small town 250–2,500   to 50,000
    ☐ large city 50,000 and over

10. What is your current marital status?
☐ single, never married   ☐ divorced, remarried
☐ married, living with spouse   ☐ widowed, not remarried
☐ separated   ☐ widowed, remarried
☐ divorced, not remarried

11. If married, did your spouse know he/she was marrying a minister or prospective minister?
☐ yes   ☐ no

12. If divorced or separated, was this a result of your being in the ministry?
☐ yes   ☐ no
If yes, please explain _____
_____
_____

13. How would you describe your spouse's attitude toward your ministry?
☐ sees him/herself as a partner in ministry
☐ is supportive of my ministry
☐ is neutral toward my ministry
☐ is opposed to my ministry
☐ other (state) _____
_____
_____

14. Do you have children?   ☐ yes   ☐ no
If yes, were they born
before you entered the
ministry?   ☐ yes   ☐ no
What are the children's ages? _____
Do you have any
stepchildren?   ☐ yes   ☐ no

15. What is/was your parents' main occupation? Please be specific.
Father _____
Mother _____

16. Were your parents
divorced/separated?   ☐ yes   ☐ no
If yes, what was your age when this occurred? _____

17. In what type community did you grow up?
☐ rural open country   ☐ small city 2,500 to 10,000
☐ village under 250   ☐ medium sized city 10,000
☐ small town 250 to 2,500   to 50,000
                              ☐ large city 50,000 and over

18. How would you describe your childhood?
☐ very happy   ☐ unhappy
☐ happy   ☐ very unhappy
☐ somewhat happy

19. In what type community did your spouse grow up?
☐ rural open country   ☐ small city 2,500 to 10,000
☐ village under 250   ☐ medium sized city 10,000
☐ small town 250 to 2,500   to 50,000
                              ☐ large city 50,000 and over

20. What was the average worship attendance of the church in which you grew up.
☐ under 25   ☐ 100–149   ☐ 350–499
☐ 25–49   ☐ 150–199   ☐ 500–999
☐ 50–99   ☐ 200–349   ☐ 1000 and over

21. What was the average worship attendance of the church in which your spouse grew up?
☐ under 25   ☐ 100–149   ☐ 350–499
☐ 25–49   ☐ 150–199   ☐ 500–999
☐ 50–99   ☐ 200–349   ☐ 1000 and over

22. Have you ever changed
denominations?   ☐ yes   ☐ no
If yes, at what age(s)? _____
If yes, what was your former denomination(s)? _____

23. Has your spouse ever
changed denominations?   ☐ yes   ☐ no
If yes, at what age(s)? _____
If yes, what was his/her former denomination(s)? _____

24. What is your annual total "salary package" (i.e., cash salary, pension, insurance, travel and other fringe benefits)?
    - ☐ under $10,000
    - ☐ $10,000–$15,000
    - ☐ $15,000–$20,000
    - ☐ $20,000–$30,000
    - ☐ $30,000–$40,000
    - ☐ $40,000–$50,000
    - ☐ over $50,000

25. Do you live in a church-owned house?   ☐ yes   ☐ no
    If yes, is the house adequate for you and your family?   ☐ yes   ☐ no

26. Is your spouse employed?
    ☐ full-time   ☐ part-time   ☐ not employed
    If employed, what is your spouse's occupation? _____

27. If employed, what is your spouse's annual income?
    - ☐ under $10,000
    - ☐ $10,000–$15,000
    - ☐ $15,000—$20,000
    - ☐ $20,000–$30,000
    - ☐ $30,000–$40,000
    - ☐ $40,000–$50,000
    - ☐ over $50,000

28. Is it necessary for your spouse to work in order for the family to make ends meet?
    ☐ yes   ☐ no

29. How would you rate your income in comparison with other pastors in your denomination with your level of experience?
    - ☐ much higher
    - ☐ somewhat higher
    - ☐ about average
    - ☐ somewhat lower
    - ☐ much lower

30. In general, do you feel that pastors in your denomination tend to be adequately paid?
    ☐ yes   ☐ no   ☐ uncertain

31. Please indicate which of the following you feel are significant advantages to being a minister. Check as many as applicable.
    - ☐ job security
    - ☐ high status in the community
    - ☐ ready-made community of friends
    - ☐ flexible schedule
    - ☐ creative work
    - ☐ spouse can participate in my work
    - ☐ support of the congregation
    - ☐ opportunities for study

☐ housing is provided
☐ support from other ministers and denomination
☐ other (state) _____

32. Please indicate which of the following you feel are significant disadvantages to being a minister. Check as many as applicable.
☐ lack of privacy
☐ financial stress
☐ living in a church-owned house
☐ being on call 24 hours
☐ unrealistic expectations of minister's spouse
☐ pressure on the children to "be perfect"
☐ unfair criticism by church members
☐ minister tends to neglect own family
☐ too heavy a work load
☐ frequent moves
☐ other (state) _____

33. How did you find the pressures associated with the ministry when you accepted your first church?
☐ less than expected
☐ about as expected
☐ greater than expected

34. Have the pressures associated with the ministry been great enough to cause you or your family members problems?
☐ yes   ☐ no
If yes, please explain _____
_____

35. How did your spouse find the pressures associated with the ministry when you accepted your first church?
☐ less than expected
☐ about as expected
☐ greater than expected

36. Does your spouse feel pressure to participate in certain local church activities?
☐ yes   ☐ no
If yes, which activities? Check.
☐ teach Sunday school class
☐ lead study groups
☐ men's/women's organizations
☐ music programs
☐ civic programs

☐ assist the minister in entertainment of church groups in the home

☐ other (list) _____

_____

_____

37. List the church activities in which your spouse participates regularly because he/she wishes to do so.

_____ _____ _____

_____ _____ _____

38. Do you take at least one full day off each week?
☐ regularly   ☐ occasionally
☐ generally   ☐ rarely

39. Do you feel that you spend an adequate amount of private time with your family?
☐ yes   ☐ no   ☐ uncertain

40. Do you regularly take a block of time for vacation?
☐ yes   ☐ no
How long was your vacation this past year? _____

41. Please indicate which of the following are problems for your family by placing a check in the appropriate space.

	a problem	sometimes a problem	not a problem
More is expected of the minister's children than other children.	☐	☐	☐
Being a clergy family isolates us from the rest of the community.	☐	☐	☐
The members expect the parsonage to be immaculate.	☐	☐	☐
There is too little privacy.	☐	☐	☐
Congregational needs have priority over family needs.	☐	☐	☐

Members have a pos-   ☐   ☐   ☐
sessive attitude about
the parsonage.
Lack of personal   ☐   ☐   ☐
friends.
Inadequate income.   ☐   ☐   ☐
Not enough time   ☐   ☐   ☐
with family.

42. What is the attitude of your denominational officials toward
     the minister's family?
     Understanding of the problems of the minister's family?
     ☐ yes   ☐ no   ☐ uncertain
     Supportive of the minister's family?
     ☐ yes   ☐ no   ☐ uncertain
     A source of problems for the minister and his/her family?
     ☐ yes   ☐ no   ☐ uncertain
     If a source of problems, please explain _____
     _____
     _____
     _____

43. Please make any comments you wish concerning the impact
     of being a minister on your family:

44. If you would be willing to talk with us by phone concerning
     the impact of the ministry on the pastor's family, please give
     your name and phone number.
                                        (   )
     _____   _____ _____
              Name   Area   Phone
                                     Code   Number

Bibliography

Bailey, Robert W. and Mary Frances Bailey. *Coping With Stress in the Minister's Home*. Nashville: Broadman, 1979.

Blackwood, Carolyn P. *The Pastor's Wife*. Philadelphia: Westminster, 1951.

Board of Higher Education and Ministry. *Clergy Family Study*. Nashville: The United Methodist Church, 1983.

Bouma, Gary. *Divorce in the Parsonage*. Minneapolis: Bethany Fellowship, 1979.

Campbell, Dennis M. *The Yoke of Obedience*. Nashville: Abingdon, 1988.

Carroll, Jackson W.; Barbara Hargrove; and Adair T. Lummis. *Women of the Cloth*. New York: Harper and Row, 1965.

Coble, Betty J. *The Private Life of a Minister's Wife*. Nashville: Broadman, 1981.

Davis, Anne and Wade Rowatt. *Formation for Christian Ministry. Review and Expositor* (1981).

Denton, Wallace. *The Role of the Minister's Wife*. Philadelphia: Westminster, 1962.

Douglas, William G. T. *Ministers' Wives*. New York: Harper and Row, 1965.

Efird, James M. *Marriage and Divorce*. Nashville: Abingdon, 1985.

Fisher, Welthy H. *Handbook for Ministers' Wives*. New York: Woman's Press, 1950.

Haines, Maxine. *This Ministry We Share: A Manual for the Wesleyan Pastor's Wife*. Marion, Ind.: Wesley Press, 1986.

Lavender, Lucille. *They Cry Too!* New York: Hawthorne, 1976.

Lawrence, Raymond J. *The Poisoning of Eros*. New York: Augustine Moore, 1989.

Lee, Cameron and Jack Balswick. *Life in a Glass House*. Grand Rapids: Zondervan, 1989.

Mace, David and Vera C. Mace. *What's Happening to Clergy Marriages?* Nashville: Abingdon, 1980.

Madsden, Keith. *Fallen Images: Experiencing Divorce in the Ministry*. Valley Forge, Pa.: Judson, 1985.

Malone, Connery. *Contemporary Perspectives on Christian Marriage.* Chicago: Loyola University Press, 1984.

Mickey, Paul. *12 Keys to a Better Marriage.* Grand Rapids: Zondervan, 1990.

————. *Breaking Free From Wedlock.* Lexington, Ky.: Bristol House, 1989.

Morgan, John Henry and Linda B. Morgan. *Wives of Priests.* Bristol, Ind.: Parish Church Library, St. John of the Cross, 1980.

Nyberg, Kathleen. *The Care and Feeding of Ministers.* New York: Abingdon, 1961.

Oden, Marilyn Brown. *The Minister's Wife Person or Position?* Nashville: Abingdon, 1966.

Rassieur, Charles. *The Problem Clergymen Don't Talk About.* (Philadelphia: Westminster, 1976.

Richards, Sue Poorman and Stanley Hagemeyer. *Ministry to the Divorced.* Grand Rapids: Zondervan, 1986.

Ross, Charlotte. *Who is the Minister's Wife?* Philadelphia: Westminster, 1980.

Sinclair, Donna M. *The Pastor's Wife Today.* Nashville: Abingdon, 1981.

Sweet, Leonard I. *The Minister's Wife.* Philadelphia: Temple University Press, 1983.

Watt, Margaret H. *The History of the Parson's Wife.* London: Faber and Faber, 1945.

Whybrew, Lyndon E. *Minister, Wife and Church: Unlocking the Triangle.* Washington, D. C.: Alban Institute, 1984.

Willimon, William H. *Clergy and Laity Burnout.* Nashville: Abingdon, 1989.